KALEIDOSCOPE OF WOMEN IN GOA

(1510-1961)

By the same author

Health and Hygiene in Colonial Goa (1510-1961)
Fatima da Silva Gracias, 1994

About the Author

Dr. Fatima da Silva Gracias has M.A. degree in History from the University of Bombay and a Ph. D. in History from the Goa University, Author of the book *Health and Hygiene in Colonial Goa, 1510-1961,* she has also contributed research papers on Health, Women and Social Institutions in Goa, in publications and research seminars in Goa and Portugal. Dr. Gracias was a recepient of a Fellowship of Fundação Oriente-Lisboa (Portugal).

KALEIDOSCOPE OF WOMEN IN GOA
1510-1961

FATIMA DA SILVA GRACIAS

CONCEPT PUBLISHING COMPANY, NEW DELHI-110059

ISBN 81-7022-591-4

First Published 1996

Published and Printed by
Ashok Kumar Mittal
Concept Publishing Company
A/15-16, Commercial Block, Mohan.Garden
NEW DELHI-110059
Phones: 5554042, 5504042

To
All Goan women
who have lived valiantly
and weathered almost untenable way of life

PREFACE AND ACKNOWLEDGEMENTS

Kaleidoscope of Women in Goa (1510-1961), contains an historical inquiry into the conditions of women in Goa, during the Portuguese rule. This is the first comprehensive work on Goan women covering the whole Portuguese period of 450 years. The work discusses the role of women in the family and in society as reflected through customs, traditions, religion, state legislation and church decrees.

The idea of undertaking this work arose in January 1992 during the visit of Dr. Mario Soares, President of the Republic of Portugal to this land.

I am indebted to Fundacao Oriente, for the award of a fellowship which enabled me to undertake research work in Goa and Portugal. My thanks and appreciation to Dr. Teotnio de Souza, Founder Director of XCHR, Porvorim, Margaret Lopes, Isabel Santa Rita Vas, Satya Costa-Ferreira and Lilia Colaco-Souza.

Several persons provided me with some useful oral information on Hindu and Muslim customs and traditions. I should mention the following in particular: Dr. Vilassini Gandolkar, Madhavi Pilgaokar, Sumedha Kamat and Dr. Salimabi, to all of them I am grateful.

I am obliged to the authorities and the staff of Historical Archives of Goa, Arquivo Nacional da Torre do Tombo, Arquivo Historico Ultramarino, Biblioteca Nacional Lisboa and Rare Books Section of Central Library, Panjim for their help and cooperation. To my family–Tagore, Rohin and Nandita, my special thanks for their continuous support and understanding!

Fatima da Silva Gracias

Panjim, Goa 1996

CONTENTS

ABBREVIATIONS

AHU	Arquivo Historico Ultramarino, Lisboa
ANTT	Arquivo Nacional da Torre do Tombo, Lisboa
APO	Archivo Portuguez- Oriental, ed. J.H. da Cunha Rivara
BNL	Biblioteca Nacional, Lisboa
BP	Bullarium Patronatus in ecclesis Africae, Asiae atque Oceaniae, ed. U. de Paiva Manso
BO	Boletim Oficial
CAA	Cartas de Afonso de Albuquerque, ed. R.A. de Bulhao Pato
COP	Cartas, Ordens e Portarias
CGSO	Conselho Geral do Santo Oficio
CD	Correspondencia Geral
DI	Documenta Indica, ed. J. Wicki
DRI	Documentos Remetidos da India (published and unpublished)
EPW	Economic and Political Weekly
HAG	Historical Archives Goa
HCIP	History and Culture of the Indian People ed. R.C. Majumdar
HD	History of Dharmashastra, ed. Kane
IG	Inquisiçao de Goa
LREI	Legislaçao Relativa ao Estado da India
PP	Paco Patriarcal, Panjim
VP	Visitas Pastorais

GLOSSARY

Words in the glossary of local vernacular derivation are indicated with Ver. The remaining terms are in Portuguese .

Aldeias: villages

Alvara: A decree issued either by the King, Viceroy or Government official and valid for one year without the royal confirmation
Bailadeira: Temple dancer
Baloes : Boats
Bairros: Quarters, wards
Bajus: Ver. Dress worn by women of upper strata
Bodki: Ver. Tonsured woman/ Hindu widow
Cabedal: Capital/funds
Cabeça de casal: Head of the family
Canarins: Native Christians of Goa
Carta regia: Royal letter
Casados: Married men/Portuguese married settlers in India.
Castiço: A person of Portuguese descent, born in Asia
Choli Ver. Tight fitting blouse worn on sari by women
Conde: Count
Conselho: Council
Cristaos Novos: New Christians, converted from Judaism
Dai: Ver. Native midwife
Degredado: Exiled.
Dolim: Ver. Means of transport used by Hindu women, priests in Goa
Dote: Dowry,gifts
Desistencia: Surrender, desistance
Estado da India: Portuguese State of India
Feitor: Factor, Crown or private trading agent
Feitoria: Factory, Crown trading post
Fidalgo: Nobleman
Firinghi rog: Ver. European disease
Ganesh Chaturti: Ver. Festival in honour of Lord Ganesh held before the harvest

Gentios: Non-Christians (Hindus and Muslims in Goa)
Goa dourada: Golden Goa
Lagna: Ver. Hindu wedding
Machila Ver. A sedan chair carried by four to six men
Meher: Ver. Bride dowry among the Muslims
Mestiços: Persons of mixed blood/a person of Indo-Portuguese ancestry
Ojims: Ver. Baskets, baskets containing foodstuff sent to married daughter
Orfas del Rei: Kings orphans
Ouvidor Geral: Senior Crown Judge
Padroado Real: The Portuguese Crown patronage of religious missions
Politica dos casamentos: Marriage policy
Prassada: Ver. Blessings, Approval
Prazos: Private Principalities,land grant on west coast of India or East Africa
Provedor: Purveyor
Pudvem: Ver. Garment worn by Hindu men.
Raibari: Ver. Middle man, marriage broker
Reinois: Portuguese born in Portugal
Recolhimento: Home for destitutes
Saguates: Gifts
Santa Casa da Misericordia: Holy House of Mercy – a charitable institution run by a brotherhood
Sati: Ver. virtuous woman/ the practice of burning on the pyre of the husband
Senado: Municipal Council
Sigmo: Ver. Hindu Festival in Goa corresponding to Holi
Soldado: Soldier,unmarried man
Solteiras: Women of easy life/unmarried women
Tanadar-Mor: Ver. Overseer/ High Government official
Tinto: Ver. Market
Tickli:Ver. A daughter born after three boys
Tesoureiro da casa de Moeda: Treasurer of the Mint
Soldo e mantimento: Basic pay and maintenance allowances
Inquisiçao de Goa: Holy Inquisition
Usos e Costumes: Usages and Customs
Kalavant:Ver. Dancing girl
Vedor de fazenda: Chief revenue superintendent
Veo Branco: White veil
Veo preto: Black veil
Xetam: Ver. Devil

INTRODUCTION

In the last few decades there is a general concern about the status and problems of women in society. Studies on women have received considerable attention from the media. Women themselves are concious about their position and roles in a mainly patriarchal society.

The UNO declared : 1975 as the *Year of the Women,* the decade 1975-85 as *Women's Decade,* 1993 as *the International Year of the Girl Child* and 1994 as the *Year of the Family,* where women play a significant role.

In this country (India) discrimination against women is apparent in dramatic and tragic ways—female infanticide, dowry crime, wife beating and widow burning. Any study of the status of women in Indian society, would have to take note of the historical development of attitudes that led to such discrimination.

The present work *Kaleidoscope of Women in Goa,* studies the theme in the Goan context. The work enquires into the status of women during the Portuguese rule in Goa. The Portuguese rule seems to have made a difference to the life style of Goan women.

Generally, whenever women are mentioned in the Indo-Portuguese Historical literature it is usually in the subordinate role of a daughter, wife, mother or a mistress. However, there are a few exceptions such as in the historical figures like Ursula Abreu (Senhora de Panjim), Isabel Fernandes (A Velha de Diu) and Dona Luiza da Silva, a wealthy widow of Cochin.

The study is based on both unpublished and published sources which include relevant Archival material available at the Historical Archives Goa, Arquivo Nacional da Torre do Tombo, Lisboa, Arquivo Historico Ultramarino, Lisboa, Arquivo da Santa Casa de Misericordia, Lisboa and Biblioteca Nacional, Lisboa.

Sources on Goan women are few, particularly about the non-Christian women. If historical literature on Hindu women is limited as far as the early period goes, historical sources pertaining to Muslim women are almost non-existent. This work had to largely depend on oral history particularly as far as customs and traditions of Goan women are concerned. Women of different communities have been interviewed with regard to their customs and performance of their rituals has been observed and noted.

The work comprises of six chapters, besides a preface, introduction, a map, appendices, a bibliography and an index.

Chapter 1 provides a picture of women in Indian society at the time of the Portuguese arrival. The chapter provides a backdrop to what follows, so that the reader specially the non-Indian reader has a preview of the conditions of women in this country when the Portuguese arrived in Goa. The chapter will also help to compare and contrast the changes brought about during the colonial times.

Chapter 2 focuses on the *Early Influences of the Portuguese Colonial rule on the status of women in Goa.* It discusses the mixed marriage policy introduced by Albuquerque, *orfas del rei,* multifaceted relations between the Portuguese men and native women, women's position in the society — including that of the *escravas,* widows and prostitutes. It also refers to ban on *sati* and some rights granted to women in the first two centuries of the Portuguese rule in Goa.

Chapter 3 is all about women as reflected through customs and folk traditions. The chapter delves with customs, traditions, Konkani proverbs and sayings concerning women in Goa. The various customs followed by Hindu, Christian and Muslim women at the time of birth, marriage and death. The chapter covers the role played by women at the major festivals, the role of nuns, *beatas, componesas, bailadeiras and solteiras.* The oral education provided to women is also touched.

Chapter 4 covers state legislation on Goan women. The benefit brought about by the Portuguese Civil Code are studied in this chapter. So are the legislation passed to prevent women from practicing non-Christian customs which were a part of their culture. The chapter also includes the prevailing *Code of Usages and Customs* of the land which were applicable to non-Christian women. The chapter describes the attempts made by the state to provide education to women.

Chapter 5 examines the responses of the Church on the conditions of women. It sketches the role of the Church in improving the conditions of women—mainly orphans, widows, fallen women and female slaves. The chapter discusses the development of institutions established by the Church to shelter women. The role of the Church and her agencies in providing education to women is referred too here.

Chapter 6 is an overview. It seeks to gather the insights and issues in the various chapters of the study. It sums up the issues examined in earlier chapters and draws some conclusions.

Appendices to the chapters provides a more detailed substantiation for statement and conclusion in this study.

1

WOMEN IN MEDIEVAL INDIA

The present chapter concerns with the conditions of women in India at the time of Portuguese arrival in Goa. The conditions of women in medieval India has been widely discussed in the modern period by historians, sociologists and those connected with studies on women. Notwithstanding, it is being dealt in this work to serve as a background to what follows and to compare the changes brought about by the Portuguese rulers in Portuguese India.

Women are indispensable to society – they have the unique power of giving birth. They were created to be mothers. Yet, the colourful half of humankind enjoyed unequal and subordinate position throughout history in India as in many parts of this globe. Traditions, scriptures and laws determined that women must always be dependent on men. The ancient Indian legalist, Manu, declared that "in childhood a female must be subject to her father, in youth to her husband, when her lord is dead to her sons; a woman must never be independent". *(Sacred Books 1967, xvi:327).* In general, women were distrusted. They were considered in those days by some men as fickle, quarrelsome and untruthful and, therefore, the need to control them.

In the early Vedic period the girls were not hated. In fact some of them were initiated in Vedic studies and were entitled to offer sacrifices to the gods. There is no reference to female infanticide in ancient times. Even if it was practiced, it must have been confined to a small section of the society (Altekar, 1987).

The Dharmashastra containing old Hindu socio-religious rules says that "a daughter was not greeted at birth, not due to any lack of love on the part of the parents, but because a daughter was a source of anxiety to them. The society expected a very high moral rectitude from women and treated lapses of men with leniency" (*History of Dharmashastra* 1974, ii:510).

There was preference for a son. Preference for a son in Indian society is immemorial. A son was prized over the girls. Vedic verses pray that, a son will be followed by more sons. A son was synonymous with economic and social benefits. He was required to continue the family line, and to perform several rituals including the last funeral rites of the parents. These rites were important for the well being of the soul. According to sacred books a brother was also required for a girl to get a husband.

The son lived with his old parents and unlike the daughter did not live in another family after marriage. "With us, the daughter is not a daughter all the days of her life. She is only a daughter until she is a wife. Then she enters into a new circle and new relationships and she literally worships a new set of Gods". (O'Molley 1976:118-119). A daughter was considered a guest in her real home even before her marriage because once married she would move to another family.

The *Atharvaveda,* one of the four *Vedas,* contains charms and rituals to ensure birth of a son in preference to that of a daughter. A verse in Atharvaveda says "Oh God ! protect my son who is to be born. Let my offspring be a man and not a woman". A mother without the son was considered as an unfortunate human being. In this kind of society the position of the woman could not have been high. There was discrimination against the daughter. Sons received better treatment, they were provided with education, nutritious food and better health care.

In medieval India the birth of a girl was generally unwelcome for several reasons. In an ordinary family, the birth of a daughter made the parents unhappy. Right from early childhood, the daughter was given to understand that she was unwanted. A daughter was not desired because of economic liabilities with regard to marriage and dowry. The birth of a daughter would eventually lead to dwindling of the family fortune. The girl was considered the root cause of misery. In those days a daughter did not contribute to the family income, and on marriage took away a portion of family fortune as a dowry. In case of poor families, parents often incurred heavy debts to marry a daughter. The birth of a second daughter was worse.

The position of women in India declined in medieval times. Women were exploited, taken for granted, suppressed and subjected to cruel rules and unreasonable customs. Women had no individuality of their own in a male dominated society. They were considered a property that could be disposed off. Throughout their life they played different subordinate roles.

Infanticide existed in certain uneducated sections of the Hindu society during the medieval period (Altekar 1987). Probably, because daughters were regarded as source of all misery and source of unending trouble by the average family, since they had to provide daughters with heavy dowry at the time of marriage.

Education

In the early period girls received some elementary education. But in medieval times the education of women was completely neglected. Girls were married very young, therefore, there was no time to educate them. Among the upper classes girls were taught to sing, dance and to play a musical instrument. Lack of education affected their all round development. The result was a gradual deterioration in their position in the society. Daughters played practically no role in the house until they were married.

Child Marriages

Marriage was well established in the medieval period. It was regarded as a social and religious necessity. A Vedic passage says that a person who was unmarried was unholy. From religious point of view an unmarried person remained unholy and not fully eligible to participate in sacraments. It was believed that a daughter should be married and not kept in the house of her father for too long, since a woman had to be a mother before she could become a complete person. The main purpose of marriage was for procreation and mainly procreation of a son.

To marry off the daughter at very early age was the custom and primarily religious duty of the father. Any departure was frowned upon by the society often leading to social ostracism.

Child marriages gained prominence in medieval times. The custom of early marriages appears to have started in the post-Vedic period, when the conditions of the Hindu society had started to deteriorate.

There are several reasons that encouraged child marriages. Child marriages were performed to protect women from the Muslim invaders. By this time a great importance was placed upon the chastity of women. It was decreed that marriages should be performed before puberty. Since it was not possible to perform marriages on the eve of puberty, marriages were performed much before the time. Sati is supposed to have encouraged child marriages in a way. It was felt that if the father of the girl died early, and the mother followed him in his funeral pyre at least there would be a husband and his family to take care of the girl.

The joint family system prevailing in India also seems to have encouraged child marriages. Since the joint family took care of the financial needs of all its earning and non-earning members, a boy could get married much before he could start to work. In addition, it was believed that a girl at early age would adjust more easily in the new family. Marriages were performed at tender age, when girls should have been sitting on their parents lap and playing with their dolls.

The reason for this difference in treatment appears to be the fact that the girls had to face greater risks in the society than an unmarried man. Public opinion also was much less sympathetic to a woman who had gone stray even unwillingly, than to a man who lead a vicious life deliberately. It was the duty of the father to marry the daughter at the right time. The presence of unmarried daughter in the house was considered inauspicious for the men of the house. The Hindus believed that a father who arranged his daughter's marriage would earn *prithvi-dana* (the gift of the earth).

When the Portuguese arrived in Goa, child marriages were popular in India. Child marriages were one of the causes of high maternal deaths at the time of delivery. During this period marriage was almost mandatory for girls. Child marriage was the root cause of the degradation of the society.

It was not unusual to marry a daughter to undesirable person, if suitable bridegroom was not found before the time of puberty. As a result, parents had to often spend heavily to marry their daughter to a person who was sometimes almost certain to discard her, to take another wife.

In medieval India, girls were married by 8 or 9 years or even earlier at the age of three or four. Young girls of pre-puberty age were many times married to men much older. Girls of 12 years were married to men 20 to 30 years their senior. The practice existed in those days not only in India, but in other places of the globe such as Brazil. This type of marriages were common specially among the girls who lacked good looks and dowry. They were married to rich old men, widowers or men of better social position than the bride.

Although, Manu prescribed that a girl of twelve should be married to a man of thirty or a man of twenty-four to a girl of eight years, at the same time he laid down that "a maiden, though of marriageable age, should rather stop in her father's house until death, than that he should ever give her to a man destitute of good qualities". This advise was often ignored by the parents who were anxious to see their daughters married before puberty.

Marriages were arranged by the parents, close relatives or friends after wide range of negotiations. The boy and the girl were not consulted regarding the choice of the partner. Their feelings were not taken into consideration. In fact they had no voice in the settlement of marriage, probably because they were too young to know their mind and to decide in this matter. In many instances the bride and the groom would see each other only after marriage.

Ajurveda emphasizes that good family famed for ten generations and freedom from diseases that are hereditary as important factors in the selection of the bridegroom. In addition, the bridegroom had to be young, intelligent, liked by the people and virile (HD 1974, ii:431). But despite this advise, the main factor that were considered were the caste and financial position of the groom. Not even enlightened families in some instances took any interest in the would be son-in-law's character or that of his family.

The Laws of Manu forbade marriages between persons of the same *gotra.* It was laid down that the bride and the groom should not be related to each other within seven generations on father's side and five generations on mother's side. The *Dharmashastra* prescribed that the wife should be at least three years younger than the husband.

It is interesting to note that men were advised to choose a wife who had an agreeable name, moderate quantity of hair on the body and head, free of physical defects, small teeth, and soft limbs. Further, he was advised not to choose a woman with thick hair on the body nor one with the name of a constellation, a tree, a river, a mountain, a bird, a snake or the one whose name inspired terror (*Sacred Books* 1967, xvi: 76-77).

A passage from Manu stated that "a twice born man"*(brahmin)* had to be careful not to choose a woman whose family avoided sacred rites, a family where *Vedas* were not studied, no male children were born and those who suffered from hemorrhoids, weakness of digestion, epilepsy, or white and black leprosy even though they were rich in kine, horses, sheep, grain or other property" (*Sacred Books,*xxv).

Preferably, daughters were married in nearby places. According to the custom, a daughter had to visit her parents on various occasions, specially in the first years of her married life. If the daughter was married in a far away place it would be difficult for her to visit her family due to lack of transport facilities.

Gifts to the Daughter at the time of Marriage

Girls were given dowry at the time of marriage. The dowry fluctuated according to the economic condition of the girl's parents and the desirability of the alliance. It was a custom among the rich to give gifts to the daughter, when she went to the house of her husband. These gifts consisted usually of animals such as cows, goats, sheep and horses. They were also given jewels, clothes, utensils and furniture. These gifts were not compulsory in the early period and were usually given out of affection for the daughter. Gifts were also given as a security to the daughter in times of need.

In medieval times, girls were given *Stridhana* – movable property consisting of jewellery, costly clothes and furniture. When the woman died her movable property would go to her children but if she died without an issue, the movable property could be claimed by her father or brothers, because normally the son-in-law would remarry.

Position of Married Woman

A married woman belonged completely to her husband and his family. She adopted her husband's *gotra*. Therefore, she was their responsibility.

The first years of marriage were often lonely for a woman as she was a stranger in her husband's home. She had not only to adjust to her husband but had also to prove herself to the women of his household. She would see her parents on a few occasions, unless she was married within the village..However, since she was young she adopted more easily to her husband's family and their ways of life.

In the social hierarchy of her new family, the bride usually occupied the lowest position. She was expected to be dutiful and submissive to the husband, parents and other elders in the joint family. Young girls at the time of marriage were advised by their mothers to look after their husbands like a demi-God. The husband was their "lord" and master *(pati)*. Therefore, the sole object of their devotion. She was to be a *pativrata* (devoted to her husband). These roles did not leave scope for self-fulfillment. The young bride was expected to show respect to her father-in-law, husband's elder brothers and refrain from talking to them. She was expected not to talk to her own husband in the presence of others.

Young wives in joint families were under complete control of their mother-in-law and other older women in the house. They went out on rare occasions – during religious festivals – accompanied by members of the family. They were expected to stay in the house for the most part of their life because seclusion prevailed among the upper classes.

Lower class women had more freedom than women of upper strata. They could go out to perform specific tasks or visit the market. However, they had to seek prior permission from the elders in the family. It was only when they grew older, that they were free to visit neighbours and attend social function on their own. Most of the time they received no sympathy from their husbands, because often they too were young or because they had no opportunity of meeting the husbands in private away from others for most part of the day.

Multiple Roles in the Family

In medieval times in India, women played multiple roles among others of a daughter, wife, mother and daughter-in-law. The role of a wife was pre-eminent.

Women were expected to have Sita (the heroine of the epic Ramayana) as their role model. Sita left the luxury in the royal palace to follow her husband in his exile. She never questioned his decisions but just abided by them. She underwent several tests, including the fire test to prove her virtue and when he abandoned her she endured her fate without protesting. Women were also meant to be like Goddess Savitri, who is well known for her extreme devotion to her husband through which she saved him from the God of death. Savitri was held as a prime example of the length to which a wife should go in aiding her husband. Ancient law books such as Laws of Manu, myths, legends, great epics Ramayana and Mahabharata as well as oral traditions encouraged and reinforced these roles.

Women were expected to be monogamous, faithful (even if the husband was not), patient, accepting and upholding all virtues. Manu says "Though destitute of virtue, or seeking pleasure (elsewhere), or devoid of good qualities, (yet) a husband must be constantly worshiped as a god by a faithful wife "(*Sacred Books* 1967, xvi: 196). The same rules did not apply for men. There were double standards in these matters. There was no excuse for adulterous women. However, adultery in men was not considered sinful. The social structure allowed men greater freedom and liberty. In another passage, Manu states

"By violating her duty towards her husband, a wife is disgraced in this world, after her death she enters the womb of a jackal and is tormented by the punishment of her sin". Hindu girls were indoctrinated with these and other teachings from a very young age. A woman could not have goals of her own beyond her house and family.

The husband had the duty to guard the wife. This was necessary as explained by Manu to preserve the purity of his offsprings and of his line.

The *Vedic* and other literature is full of rules of conduct for a married woman. It imposed several restrictions on her and made her subservient to the husband and members of his family. A married woman had to be modest in her clothes and ways.

Rules of conduct in the house were prescribed for the wife. For instance, she was expected to rise before her husband and eat after him. The wife could not call the husband by his name. This respect was necessary as it was believed it would give longevity to the husband. According to ancient literature a married woman was not permitted to talk to men outside the family circle. Manu declared that "a faithful wife, who desires to dwell (after her death) with her husband must never do anything that might displease him, whether he be alive or dead." (*Sacred Books* 1967, xvi: 332-335).

A woman had to be submissive and devoted to her husband in any and every circumstance. It was maintained that a woman who controlled her thoughts, speech and action, would gain in her life the highest renown and in the next world a place near her husband.

The husband could not completely guard his wife, but he could guard her by employment of the following: "Let the (husband) employ his (wife) in the collection and expenditure of his wealth, in keeping (everything clean), in (the fulfilment of) religious duties, in the preparation of his food, and in looking after the household utensils" says the Laws of Manu. (*Sacred Books,* xvi: 329).

In medieval times the family was the main concern of a woman. She was advised not to pay attention to her looks neither to the looks of her prospective husband. She was expected to give herself to any kind of man without considering his physical attributes. "She who, controlling her thoughts, words and deeds, never slights her lord, resides after death with her husband in heaven and is called a virtuous wife" (*Sacred Books,* xvi:197).

During this period a variety of rituals were performed by the wife and the mother primarily for the good health of the husband and their children. A wife who did not observe these rites was believed to neglect her husband and she was looked down by the family and the society. A woman was honoured within the home. Manu says that "women must be honoured and adorned by their fathers, brothers and husbands who desire their own welfare". It was believed that if women were honoured Gods were pleased. Women were honoured on holydays and festivals with gifts of ornaments, clothes and food. They were honoured not for their own sake but due to the fear that they would destroy men when not honoured. Manu declared that the house on which female relations were not duly honoured, would perish completely as if destroyed by magic. At the same time Manu laid down that the husband had absolute rights over the wife to the extent of inflicting corporal punishment and could discard her immediately if she said anything disagreeable to him.

Early marriages were followed by early maternity. They contributed also to high fertility rate. Married couples had large families for several reasons including socio-economic factors.

Desire for sons forced women into unwanted pregnancies. High infant and child mortality due to lack of medical facilities, malnutrition and hygiene led to economic necessity of bearing many children so that some may survive to provide much needed manual labour in agriculture. More births were needed to ensure surviving adults when the parents become old. Several pregnancies were responsible for maternal death among women.

The position of a woman improved once she became a mother and mainly the mother of a son. It conferred upon her a purpose and identity. The mother was revered. The son had to protect the mother even if she was despised by the society. A woman who failed to give birth to a boy was often ill treated by her husband's family and in some communities forced to get rid of daughters soon after birth.

As mother she played an important role in the upbringing of her children and in transmitting to them certain values. The family traditions concerning child care were transmitted to the young mother by her own mother, mother-in-law or an elderly member of the family. Sometimes the midwife played an important role in providing information about child care. Girls were trained to be good mothers from a young age. Child care was considered an important part of a girl's life, therefore, she was frequently asked to look after babies in the joint family.

Women of lower strata in addition to traditional roles of a wife, housewife and mother contributed often to the family income. She did all household duties which included cooking, cleaning, looking after the children, fetching water, making mats, and collection of cowdung. These women assisted men in the traditional occupation like cultivation. This situation is still true even today. Women earned half the wages earned by men for an equivalent day's work not because of her productivity was less but due to cultural attitudes, practices and power structures in a society. Woman of lower income group worked out of necessity irrespective of family responsibility. She received no help from her husband in household tasks.

The upper class women looked after their homes and a few managed household affairs. The daily expenditure of the house was regulated by them. Their outside needs were taken care by male members of the family or people employed to help them.

A woman was seldom granted rights as an individual with one notable exception that is as a mother-in-law. She could exercise some status, authority and mobility in her own right. The house work was assigned by the mother-in-law to the daughters-in-law. The share of the youngest daughter-in-law was the greatest. Sometimes they hardly received any consideration from various members of the family.

Childless Women

Women who did not have children were almost despised by the society. The glance of such women was feared as it was assumed that they would bring evil to other people's children. Barren women were inauspicious guest at a wedding and other ceremonies. Women themselves used to feel unfulfilled because they had not given birth to a child. Several herbal medicine were prescribed for women to bear children. Childless women visited temples, places of pilgrimages as well as shamans.

Purdha

Purdha came into existence with the advent of Islam in India. *Purdha* prevailed among women of the upper strata of the society. They were expected to cover their face. Even if they did not cover their face they had to follow certain code of behavior before men including male members of the joint family. Restrictions were imposed on their movements outside the house.

Women of the lower strata who could not forego women's earning in the field were not following purdha. But when a formerly poor family became prosperous, its women were quite ready to adopt more stringent seclusion, partly because it relieved them from grinding work for wages. Purdha not only entitled covering of women's face but included restrictions on her movements outside the house and respectful demeanor within the home.

Women were required to behave modestly restrained in speech and in movement. They had to avoid eye-contact with males, avoid loud speech, laughter and limit conversation with non-family males to necessary work connected topics. Women had to veil before the senior men in the family. They had to cover their heads at the approach of an older man of their husband's family using either the end of her *sari* or a head scarf known as *dupatta* .

It was believed that purdha was the direct result of the Muslim rule. Initially, the custom was observed in certain royal families and it began to be imitated by families in higher and fashionable society. It was accepted by the Hindus partly as an additional protection for women from the eyes of the Muslim conqueror.

Monogamy

Monogamy normally prevailed in medieval India, but there are references to polygamy mainly among the upper strata. Men, of upper classes particularly the royal family had many wives or kept mistresses some from among the dancing girls. It was assumed, that the inclination for men to go to several women was natural. Men enjoyed much more freedom in sexual matters than women. The duty of a devoted wife was to accept the situation and to try to prevent it if possible. The onus was always on the women. Vedic literature is full of references to polygamy. They prescribe several charms to win back the husband and for causing estrangement between him and the co-wife. According to Manu a woman could have only one husband.

A man could supersede his wife by another on various grounds. He could leave his wife if he found that she committed adultery, or was not a virgin at the time of marriage. A man was permitted to seek another wife if the previous one was mischievous, wasteful, rebellious, suffered from a incurable disease or was addicted to alcohol. However, the wife could not do so on similar grounds. In case a wife failed to give birth to a child, the husband had to wait for eight years to see if the wife could give birth to a child before marrying again. He had to wait for ten years, if the wife gave birth to still born children, and twelve years if she gave birth to daughters only. A man who disobeyed these rules had to pay the wife gratuity, *stridhana,* money and a fine to the ruler. Kautilya says that "a man may marry several wives after giving sulka and *stridhana* to those whom nothing had been given at the time of marriage". He believed that women were married for procreating sons. Therefore, when she could not give birth to a son, the husband could have another wife.

In order to remarry, according to Manu, the husband had to seek the consent of the previous wife. This was a mere formality. In practice, permission of the wife was not sought and even when it was sought most wives could not deny the same, since they were not economically independent. In fact, they were expected to live in the home of the husband in case they could not live with their parents. If she decided to live with her parents, she could not claim any maintenance.

Kautilya's Arthasastra was more considerate towards women as far as divorce or separation was concerned "if a husband either is of bad character, or is long gone abroad, or has become a traitor to his king, or is likely to endanger the life of his wife, or has fallen from his caste or has lost virility, he may be abandoned by his wife"(HCIP, II: 565). Few wives in practice left their husbands. They found it difficult to do so due to socio-economic problems.

Sati – An Ancient Custom

Sati – the practice of burning the wife in the pyre of her dead husband was prevalent predominantly among high caste Hindus. These immolations were sometimes voluntary and did not exist in the Vedic period. One of the first reference to sati appears in the great epic *Mahabharata.* The practice began among the Rajputs and was followed by wives and concubines.

Why did a woman become a *Sati? Sati* literally means virtuous. Married women were expected to be loyal to their husbands even after the death of the husbands. Among the Hindus of upper strata women were encouraged to become *sati* – by burning in the pyre of their husbands, many times against the wishes of these women. According to the brahmins, marriage was a bond that could not be dissolved even after the death of the husband. This applied only to women. Hindu men could remarry after the funeral of the wife and even have many wives or concubines. Dying with the husband was considered an act of glory and virtue for a woman. It was the duty of the wife to die with her husband. In a male dominated society a woman had no importance without the husband.

Women who committed *sati* were acclaimed as goddesses and honoured with shrines and rituals. Apparently, a reward to encourage other women to follow the example. The practice was followed among the upper classes, probably because these women were not economically independent. They had no right to their husband's property. Widows had to be dependent on members of the family. A common belief was that *sati* conferred great blessings on the husband and the wife in the next life. Generally, women had no courage to defy the practice but few who resisted the practice were dragged and pushed with long stakes after having been bathed, ritually attired and intoxicated with opium or alcoholic drinks. The feelings of these women were not considered. In spite the nature of the custom, sometimes women voluntarily and with great delight died with their husbands.

Special funeral arrangements were made in the case of a *Sati,* so that the woman did not recoil. The funeral pyre was piled in a deep pit to make her escape impossible. The woman, dressed in ceremonial clothes, was escorted to the pyre by her relatives who chanted a song in praise of her virtue. When the sati approached the pyre, she took off all her ornaments and distributed them among the various members of the family and friends. Then she was helped by her brother or other member of the family on to the pyre.

Traditionally, it was believed that sati increased the honour and prestige of the family and the clan. Marriage was considered as indissoluble union even in the other world. *Sati* was practiced not only in India but also in some other parts of Asia. *Sati* was considered by some women in India as a better alternative to a miserable life of a widow.

Conditions of Widows

Child marriages often led to early widowhood. Widowhood was the alternative to *sati.* Girls were many times married to men much older than them, consequently, many of them became widows at a very young age. Widows were not permitted to remarry. While Laws of Manu forbade widow remarriages, another ancient text *Narada-smriti* permitted the same. However, widows were reluctant to remarry due to the attitude of the society towards such marriages. Therefore, a widow preferred to die with her husband rather than remain a widow.

Widows were inhumanly treated after the death of their husbands.

In fact, they were at times blamed for the death of the husband. Widowhood was regarded as retribution for crimes committed in an earlier life. Scant regard was shown to the widows. Upper class widows were in a particular vulnerable position since they were restricted from obtaining employment outside the home and were also forbidden to remarry. Generally, they were subject to neglect, maltreatment and made helpless victims of sexual abuse.

Widows were placed in greater dependence on their families. They were expected to live a secluded life. Restrictions were imposed on their clothing, movement and diet. Tradition demanded they should wear white clothes, live a simple life and eat plain food. Their heads were shaved to make them less attractive and prevent them from marrying again. They were expected to spend their time praying, fasting or working in the kitchen.

Widowhood was a dreary life of enforced celibacy. It was believed that the women who remained chaste after the death of their husbands would reach heaven. The society did not show much sympathy to the widows. Some of them in order to escape this dreary life led an immoral life. *Sati* began to appeal more to all classes of the society. If the widow continued to live in her husband's home she had to work like a slave, if she lived separately she was given very little for her maintenance and would loose respect in the society. She had to spend her life with her head and arms bared. She was an outcaste ,on festive occasions – a bad omen. Therefore, not allowed even to attend the marriage of her own children.

Tavernier, an European traveller who visited India, says that priests encouraged women to commit *Sati* with the hope that at the moment they are in the fire Rama (God) will reveal wonderful things to them (priests).

The ideal of *pativrata* strongly rejected any consideration of remarriage of a widow. Widow remarriage was not encouraged by the society. But some widows could have children by niyoga (levirate). This usually happened when a man died without a son. It was the duty of the brother-in-law to see that a son was born to his sister-in-law in order to perpetuate the memory of his brother. He was permitted to have sexual relations with her until a child was born. While women were discouraged from remarriage, widowers were sought after matches for young girls.

Women and Property Rights

The Hindu law gave unequal and indifferent treatment to women. They were discriminated against in marriage, divorce, widowhood and inheritance.

In a joint Hindu family, the father was the head of the family. Sons acquired right to their father's property soon after birth. Girls could not inherit their paternal property. They were entitled only to maintenance but a widow without a son had a share in the property.

Married women had no right on their husbands' property and even their home. After the death of the husband often they were thrown out of their husbands' home and forced to seek shelter with brothers or relatives in whose house they were treated as servants. When things became unbearable, they left these relatives and became prostitutes.

The above survey shows that women in medieval India enjoyed a subordinate position in the family and the society. She was made dependent on men and deprived of her rights.

2

EARLY INFLUENCES OF PORTUGUESE COLONIAL RULE ON THE STATUS OF WOMEN

In this chapter we embark on our bird's-eye view of women in Goan society in the first century of the Portuguese rule. Goa before the Portuguese came to India, was under the control of various Hindu and Muslim rulers. The Portuguese conquered Goa in 1510 from Adilshah, a Muslim ruler. The conditions of women in Goa at this time were the same as those of their counterparts elsewhere in India. The duties of women far exceeded their non-existent rights. The Portuguese rule seems to have made the difference as far as the conditions of the women are concerned.

Albuquerque who laid the foundation of the Portuguese empire in India, showed some concern with the position of the women in Goa. Albuquerque's successors too contributed to improve the status of women in the society. As a result the position of women in Goa was better than that of their counterparts in other parts of India, where *sati,* female infanticide and other negative practices prevailed. Goan women were given the right to their father's property in the first century of the Portuguese rule in Goa. Elsewhere in India women had no right to family property until the middle of the twentieth century.

In the first century of the Portuguese rule, the State and the Church introduced reforms to improve the conditions of women. Reforms were introduced to do away with some negative cultural practices existing in our society, such as *sati.* Widows were encouraged to remarry. During this period laws were passed giving women some rights, mainly property rights. These rights were extended with certain reservations. Initially for women who converted to Christianity, and later to non-Christian women.

Foreign travel accounts, starting with Tome Pires, provide us with interesting information about the conditions of the women in Goa and mainly in the city of Goa. The conditions of the women in our society depended on their social/cultural/religious position. The division of society was not watertight. There was some mobility during the period.

The caste system existed among the Hindus.The society was divided in four castes-*Brahmins, Kshatryias, Vaisyas* and *Sudras.* When some of these Hindus were converted to Christianity, they continued with this system. Nevertheless, for the purpose of this study the society is divided mainly on religious basis rather than as per the caste system. Broadly speaking, women in the Goan society could be placed in two groups: Christian women and non-Christian women.

Christian women were further divided into: (a) Reinois, castiças and mestiças (b) Native Christian women. Reinois were the ones who came from Portugal. This class included the wives of the officials, orfas del Rei sent from Portugal to marry Portuguese men in India and a few others such as *aventureiras* who came to India on board of Portuguese ships. The number of Portuguese women in Goa was very small in the early period. *Castiças* were those born to Portuguese parents in India and mestiças who were of mixed blood. *Mestiças* were looked down upon by *reinois* and *castiças.* These too were a small group. Women born of a union between the Portuguese and a black were known as *mulatas.* Portuguese women and those of mixed blood were less traditional than the native women. They had a comfortable life style.

Native Christian women were those who were converted to Christian religion, and their progeny. The life style of these women depended on their economic conditions. The upper and the middle class women were more traditional than those women who belonged to the lower strata.

Non-Christian women were in a majority. Non-Christian women included Hindus and Muslims. Among the Portuguese they were known as *gentias.* Just like their Christian counterparts their conditions too depended on their economic status.They were traditional in their ways. In addition, the city of Goa was inhabited by women of various nationalities including the *banya* women who belonged to dominant trading community from Gujarat and the slave women.

A Politica dos Casamentos

Albuquerque is well known for his encouragement of mixed marriages between his men and native women. Immediately, after taking over Goa, Albuquerque started with the policy known as *Politica dos Casamentos* (Marriage Policy) of getting what G.V. Scammel calls the "Lusitanian rank and file" married to local women. (Scammel 1989:170). They were mainly soldiers, masons, carpenters, artisans and similar low rank people. (Figueiredo-Correia Afonso 1933:42). Many of these men were *degredados* (convicts-exiled from Portugal). *Comentarios do Grande Albuquerque* mentions that the *Tesoureiro de Casa de Moeda* (Treasurer of the Mint) and other officials were married to native women (CGAA,iii:49). These must have been a few exceptions. Two months after the conquest of Goa, Albuquerque had arranged about two hundred mixed marriages. (G. Correia, i:443).

Politica dos Casamentos was a pragmatic one. The primary motive of this *Politica dos Casamentos* was to create a white identity in India which would help to perpetuate the Portuguese rule in the Estado da India–a new community that would form the backbone of Portuguese power in Asia. A community that would be loyal to Portugal and happy to be in this region.

Portugal had a small population at this time and she could not afford to send large numbers of soldiers to India. The mortality rate among the soldiers and other Portuguese travellers to India was high. Many died on the way due to diseases such as scurvy and high fevers caused by lack of medical care, proper diet and water. Many others succumbed to diseases in Goa. (Silva Gracias, 1994). The extent of female imigration from Portugal to India was low throughout the sixteenth century.

Albuquerque gave economic incentives to his men to marry native women. He endowed them with dowry in cash and kind. Each couple was granted 18,000 *reis,* a house, cattle, land and all that was necessary to start a new home.(CGAA, iii:50). Thus, for instance in 1511 the captain of Goa Diogo Mendes Vasconcelos and *feitor* Francisco Corvynell were ordered to give Pedro Vas a sum of 10,000 *reis* as part of his dowry. (CAA,vi:456). Another man Francisco Abexim was granted at the time of his marriage 6,000 *reis,* silk cloth, rice and some other commodities. Albuquerque ordered also that Joao Rodrigues, a mason by profession should be given at the time of his marriage 16,000 *reis* in silver or gold so that he could make jewellery for his wife.(CAA, vi:286). Fernão de Basto was provided at the time of marriage with *dezoito mil reis* and a slave woman.(CAA,v:265). Francysco Vyera, married to Guimar d'Albuquerque, a maid servant of the Governor, was given merces, 20,000 *reis,* a house and a job. Men marrying native women were given minor government posts such as the post of a *tanadar, tabeliao,* a post in the Municipal Council or even helped to start some business. In case a woman asked for the house that belonged to her parents that too was given to her. (Commentarios, 1973, i:49). *Degredados* who married native women were given *soldo e mantimento.* If they complained about another man eying their wives, such a man was exiled to another place. (G. Correia 1923, i: 49).

There was a rather odd incident, where Albuquerque got several couples married in a private home. The place was poorly lit and overcrowded. In the confusion Portuguese men took the wrong wives homes and tried to exchange them for the right ones the next morning.(Barros 1945,ii/ 243, Silva Gracias 1994).

Some sources state that the first women to be married to the Portuguese men were Muslim women abandoned by their parents and husbands during the conquest of Goa by the Portuguese (Figueiredo-Correia Afonso 1933). However, Sanjay Subrahmanyam, in his work *The Portuguese Empire in Asia* remarks "only a few of these–those associated with soldiers and administrators from the proceeding Adil Shahi administration–are likely to have been fair Mooresses". (Subrahmanyam 1993:220).

Except for captive Brahmin women, generally women who married these Portuguese men could not have been high class women. Hindus of upper classes did not encourage inter-caste marriages.(Boxer 1963:77) During the later period even *mestiços* were reluctant to marry their daughters to Portuguese men because those in Goa were either useless soldiers or grand and haughty.(Abbe Carre 1990: i/191). Besides, Hindu girls were married very young . It appears that the majority of women married to Portuguese during early period were low caste women who had been converted to Christianity. There are few instances when Albuquerque arranged marriages between Portuguese men of good character and daughters of well known native families. But this excluded the dark Malabari women, although many of them were good looking and rich.

Albuquerque appears to be conscious of colour and complexion. He was careful to advise his men not to marry dark Malabari women. He encouraged them to marry fair and chaste Muslim women.(CAA ,I:337-338). The Muslim women in turn preferred the Portuguese, because of better treatment given to them and the general belief among these women that conversion to Christianity would absolve them of their sins. However, high class Nair women were not prepared to marry Portuguese men but the Canarin women readily accepted alliances with the Portuguese.

In the beginning of Portuguese rule there was a great demand from Portuguese soldiers for mixed marriages. Albuquerque could not satisfy the demands of his men. In the early period, parents of the native girls were reluctant to marry off their daughters but when they realized that the Portuguese men treated them well, they came forward to marry them off. Many of them believed also that if they married white people their race would become lighter skinned (Thevenot and Careri 1949:187). These people formed a class by themselves. Portuguese men married to native women were known as *casados.* They were granted special privileges and had separate quarters *(bairros)* usually in urban areas.

After all that has been said the number of Portuguese whites married to local women was never too large. The figures for *casados* in Goa are difficult to determine. In 1600 an estimate of about 6000 *casados* is given for Portuguese Asia. A. Disney has reckoned that the number of *casados* remained stable from about the middle of the sixteenth century into the first and second decade of the seventeenth century, averaging nearly 2,000.(Disney 1978). In 1635 there were about 800 white *casados* in Goa.(Subrahmanyam 1993). A mixed marriage policy was followed in Cochin too.

Albuquerque was disappointed to find that many times his men married native women for money and other incentives. Albuquerque called native women married to Portuguese, his daughters, and the men were known as his sons-in-law.

Albuquerque's *Politica dos Casamentos* helped in a way to legalize some casual relationships that the Portuguese men had with native women. Mixed marriage policy of Albuquerque, met with opposition from his own country men including the clergy and some Government officials among them was Diogo Mendes de Vasconcelos. They tried to undermine the entire mixed marriage project. As a result, there was dissatisfaction among the *casados* of Goa, some of whom contributed towards the growing opposition and instigated by their native wives at one point joined the conspiracy to hand over Goa to the Muslims.

A decline in mixed marriages was noticed after 1519.(Ferreira Martins 1932). The policy was not pursued by Albuquerque's immediate successors. Soldiers and others who came to India preferred to have casual relations with local women including the beautiful slaves rather than to marry them. At the end of the seventeenth century the State tried once more to promote mixed marriages between Portuguese men and native women. Viceroy Francisco de Tavora, Conde de Alvor issued an *alvara* in 1684 for the purpose.

Native women who married Portuguese whites embraced the Christian religion. Some of their parents too converted to the religion of their daughters, although many of them continued privately to practice their own rituals. They were influenced by western culture and learnt to speak the Portuguese language. These marriages led to the mingling of cultures – eastern and western.

Multifaceted Relations

Given the fact that in the sixteenth century the Portuguese men largely outnumbered Portuguese women in Goa, it is not surprising that the Portuguese were involved in all kinds of relations with native women.

In the sixteenth and seventeenth centuries it was a custom among the Portuguese whites to migrate generally without their women to Brazil, West Africa or Asia. Apparently, the State discouraged men to take their wives to far away lands but at times made provisions to send *orfas del Rei* to Asia.

The number of women who came to Goa Dourada was much lower than those who migrated to Brazil, probably because Brazil offered better prospects. In addition to *orfas del Rei, aventureiras* and a few others came to India in this period.

The low female immigration to the East, says C. R. Boxer, had something to do with finances. The average male emigrant could not afford to take his wife and daughters to India without monetary grants *(ajuda do custo)* from the Crown which were difficult to come by. (Boxer 1975). Many men were sent to India on punitive grounds. In addition, long journeys to the East, the hot climate and prevalence of diseases must have also discouraged Portuguese women from coming to Portuguese Goa.

Since Portuguese men came to India without their wives, it created several social problems. Majority of the *Fidalgos* were married in their home country but they would leave behind their legitimate wives and keep mistresses in Goa and other parts of Portuguese India.(Conde de Ficalho 1886). Many of these *fidalgos* and Government officials had lasting relationships with *bailadeiras.* Inquisidores were also accused of having relationships with these women. (ANTT: CGSO-IG, 31/2). Even the viceroys left their wives behind in Portugal. In mid eighteenth century Marchioness of Tavora was the first wife of a viceroy who was granted permission by the Portuguese ruler to travel to Goa. When she sailed with her husband she created a sensation in Lisbon's political and social circles.

The society of the time was promiscuous. The Portuguese, for the most part deprived of the company of women of their own race, associated with all kinds of *mestiço* and native women regardless of their marital status – unmarried, married, widows and *solteiras.* It was said at the end of the sixteenth century that *fornicar no es pecado* (Boxer 1975). Life in the city of Goa was ceaséless round of amorous assignments and sexual delights according to some available accounts.

Information available refers to amorous activities of the Portuguese men and native women, what Afonso de Albuquerque termed "living in sin". Albuquerque complains in one of his letters that the Portuguese men carried women along with them out of Goa . However, there are instances when he sent women for the use of Portuguese men. In a letter dated 1513 Albuquerque informs the Factor of Goa, that he was sending eight women for the use of Portuguese men and that they should be looked after well and paid. He further mentioned that in four months time, these women would be replaced by new ones from Cananor. There appears to have been double standards in these matters. Many times , Portuguese men took women to the ships for casual sex, termed by Albuquerque as "infernal play". Apparently, all hell broke loose in such occasions (Silva Gracias 1994).

European travellers, namely Linschoten, Pyrard, Manucci and others who visited Goa in the sixteenth and seventeenth centuries of the Portuguese rule make pointed references to male sexual laxity as well as considerable sexual license on the part of women. The Dutch traveller Linschoten, who visited Goa in the late sixteenth century described women as " luxurious and unchaste"(Linschoten 1988, i: 209). In the 16th century adulterous women thrown out by their husbands sought shelter in Churches or moved to the enemy kingdom. The situation was responsible for several problems leading Viceroy Dom Antao de Noronha to issue an *alvara.* The *alvara* advised women seeking shelter at the Church to apply to the *Ouvidor Geral da India* to provide accommodation at the homes of honest married gentlemen until they could be sent to the *Casas do Coutos* of Cananor or Daman. (HAG: Ms 8691-RG-IG 78-79 v).

Pyrard, the French traveller of early seventeenth century provides us a colourful account of women in the city of Goa. He describes how upper-class married ladies (Portuguese, *mestiças* and some others) drugged their husbands with *Dutro* so that they could have freedom with their lovers (Pyrard 1944, ii: 87). *Dutro* or *Datura* was a herb available in Goa which produced a fruit. The sap mixed with some drink or meat stock was used to intoxicate to the extent that the person who drank the same would be completely drugged and unaware of his surroundings. The person could remain so for several hours or until he was revived by washing his feet. In the meantime the wives would have a good time with their lovers in the same room. Men used this drug also to poison and get rid of their adulterous wives. According to Linschoten, such men in order to be absolved of the crime would cut the throat of their wives. Then they would get four witnesses to testify that it was done by strange men who entered the house to have pleasure with their wives. But this did not deter the wives from carrying extramarital relationships. In order to increase their libido these women ate condiments such as cloves, pepper, ginger and an extract of ganja. They also gave similar mixtures to their husbands to satisfy their desires.

In 1616 *inquisodores* of the Holy Inquisition were requesting the Portuguese ruler to stop the ambassador of the Adil Shah from taking young girls from Goa for the use of his ruler.(ANTT:CGSO-IG: 121v-122).

The World of Solteiras

The word *solteira* in the early period meant a woman of easy life. Today this word has different connotation and means spinster. Prostitution was widespread in the early period. The vice was responsible for sexually transmitted diseases including syphilis which was common in Goa during Portuguese rule.(Silva Gracias,1994:91).

In the early period of Portuguese rule prostitutes were found all over the city of Goa, and particularly in an area known as *Ilha de Fogo*. Lower class Indian prostitutes were commonly known among the Portuguese as *perrinhas malabares.* Several measures were taken to curb the activities of these women. These measures are discussed elsewhere in this work. The nautch girls from mainland were found at the island of Kumbarjua. The Jesuits who collected a tax from the prostitutes in this area, were accused of encouraging the trade. Many of these prostitutes in the city of Goa were called home by their clients. High class prostitutes and adulterous women were found moving in closed palanquins and soliciting from house to house. In 1567 the Municipality of Goa was advised by the Church Provincial Council to fix certain areas for prostitutes beyond the Hospital of St. Lazarus at the city of Goa.

Orfas del Rei –Prospective Brides

Orfas del Rei were young orphan girls who were sent from orphanages of Lisbon, Porto and some other places of Portugal to India at the expense of the Crown. *Orfas del Rei* were sent annually to India as potential spouses to Portuguese men living in Estado da India in order to increase the white population in this region. In their own country the authorities had problems getting these girls married due to lack of sufficient dowries. Ferreira Martins mentions that *orfas del Rei* were sent to India at the request of Viceroys who were keen on preventing mixed marriages between Portuguese men and native women. Interestingly, there are instances when orphan del Rei married native men. In mid sixteenth century the ruler of Maldives (who had converted to Christianity) married D.Francisca de Vasconcelos, an orphan who had come from Portugal (Figueiredo-Correia Afonso 1933).

There is difference of opinion about the number of orphans that were sent annually to India. Germano Correia states that they were sent in large numbers to India. According to him in the *armada* that left Tejo in April 1584 hundreds of orphan girls travelled to India (Germano Correia MCMXLVIII) while C.R. Boxer, the historian of Portuguese empire contests this assessment. Boxer feels that five to fifteenth would have been more likely annual figure (Boxer, 1975:66). More recently, Sanjay Subrahmanyam states that about ten orphan girls came to India annually (Subbrahmanyam:1993).

The first batch was sent to India in 1545 and it continued in the next two centuries. In 1595 the Portuguese Crown temporarily stopped the dispatch of these girls, probably as result of complaints sent by the authorities in Goa. These authorities found it difficult to settle *orfas del Rei,* since in addition they had to look after the orphans whose fathers had died fighting for the Crown in Estado da India. In the same year a royal *alvara* decreed that the privileges granted to *orfas del Rei* were also to be extended to orfas whose father died fighting for the Crown in India.(HAG: Ms. 8793- RG-LV,3/129-129v.). *Orfas del Rei* were sent to India at the care of *Santa Casa da Misericordia de Goa.* It was the responsibility of this institution to arrange suitable accommodation for these girls with honest families until they could be married. *Santa Casa da Misericordia de Goa* maintained them, the same way as was done for instance by *Santa Casa da Misericordia* of Cochin (South India) and Colombo (Sri Lanka).

Towards the end of sixteenth century there were complains from the *Inquisidores* of Goa that the Viceroys were getting some *orfas del Rei* from noble families married to Portuguese of Jewish origin settled in the *Provincias de Norte.*

During the same period, the Viceroys of India were writing to their King not to send orphan girls to Goa as there many yet to be married and there was no place to accommodate them(APO, i: 81 and 109). The difficulty in arranging accommodation for these girls with respectable families led Archbishop Dom Aleixo de Menezes to establish a home for them.

Orfas del Rei were provided with dowry and jobs for the men prepared to marry them. Their husbands were given the charge of *Feitorias Fortalezas and Prazos* mainly in the *Provincias do Norte*– Daman, Diu, Chaul, Bassein, Salsette and other minor centres.The second husband of D. Catarina Antunes de Melo was granted the captancy of Daman fort for three years (Germano Correia,v: 103). However, grant of captaincies of *Fortalezas* was subject to Royal confirmation.(AHU: India-Caixa 20/58). Isabel de Melo Teixiera de Azavedo, daughter of Mateus de Azavedo and D. Catarina Antunes de Melo, married to Luis de Merinha Henriques was granted the charge of Rachol fort for a *trienio* (three years). Jeronimo de Melo, husband of Vitoria Mesquita, was appointed as Guardamor of Diu. A royal decree dated 1583 permitted the Viceroys to grant trading agencies to men marrying these orphans provided these men were qualified.

It must be noted that despite reasonable dowries, and the best efforts of *Misericordia*, Viceroys and *Senado* (Municipal Council) not all girls found suitable husbands. Most lacked good looks or were old and sickly. During the time of Conde de Redondo a cash grant of 1000 *xerafins* was added to minor government post to help the couple to set up a home.(HAG: MR-28B). In 1627 we have Conde de Vidigueira again asking the Crown to further supplement grants in cash as the prospective husbands were no longer interested in just minor government posts. In the second half of the seventeenth century, *aldeias the Provincias de Norte* were in great demand as a part of dowry for orphan girls. These *aldeias* were granted subject to the condition that the girls should marry *reinois* (Portuguese whites). The grants were made by the Crown for two to three lifetimes in return for the payment of an annual *foro,* maintenance of Arab horse and a musket for local defence. The grantee had to reside in the concerned *aldeia* (Boxer 1975).

Child Marriages

Child marriages continued to prevail among the natives. Linschoten writes "when woman is seven years old, and the man nine years, they do marrie, but they come not together before the woman bee strong enough to bear children" (Linschoten, i: 249). This statement was corroborated by Tavernier (Tavernier 1977:197). Another European traveller, the Italian Manucci tells us that the girls were married before the age of ten (Manucci, iii: 59-60). Marriage as in other parts of India was not consummated before the girl reached puberty. Somehow it was the duty of the parents to get their daughters married before they reached puberty for the same reasons as in the rest of India. Hindu girls were married usually within the caste. Intercaste marriages were rare among the native particularly of upper classes.

Women and Education

Since girls were married off early, they received no formal education. Education was not available to them. They were trained in home arts. Christian girls received religious education at Church and at home. They attended cathecism classes (DI,viii:61). Young novices at the Convent of Santa Monica were taught to read and to write in Portuguese and to sing hymns. These novices learnt also Latin and all that was necessary to be a nun. These nuns were good at handicraft.

Hindu girls were provided religious education at home. Some of them also learnt to sing. Hindu women of *Kalavant* class learnt to sing and dance to the beat of *murdanga*. In the later period they learnt to read and to write.

Social Life

Women of upper strata of all communities seldom went out except on festive occasions (Pyrard:ii/78). Christian women went to the Church on feast days, to attend a marriage or christening. They moved out well guarded in a covered palanquin (not to be seen), accompanied by other members of the family and a vast retinue of slaves. Each slave was in charge of various things required by the mistress at the Church such as carpet, cushions, chair, prayer book, paper fan and a rosary. One of the slaves had the duty of fanning the lady. Women of upper strata sat separately from others.

When they went out, women of upper strata wore costly apparels of velvet, damask, brocade and satin adorned with pearls and precious stones. Some of these textiles were imported from China and other places. At times apparel was embroidered with gold thread. Silk was cheap. It was even used by slaves on festive occasions. Women of upper classes wore on their feet very high heeled *chapins,* open in the upper side. The lower part was embroidered with gold and silver spangles studded with precious stones and pearls. Since the footwear was very high, they needed help of one or two persons to walk from the palaquin to the Church. Their only concession to heat was that they wore no stockings. They spent large sums on beautiful jewellery made of gold and adorned with precious stones.

Native Christian women of upper and middle class wore *pano-bajus* or *saris. Bajus* were also known as *toropo baju.* This apparel as worn by some women in Goa even in the first fifty years of the twentieth century. It consisted of a loose blouse and a piece of cloth about 2 meters long which was wrapped around the waist and gave an appearance of a long skirt with two front pleats.

Saris were worn along with a tight fitting *cholis* or blouses. A decree issued by the Holy Inquisition in the eighteenth century forbade Christian women to wear *cholis.* (ANTT:CGSO- IG-36/23). Many of the Christian women wore *hol* when they went to Church. *Bajus* were replaced by western style clothes in the last century of the Portuguese rule in Goa. Due to excessive heat women wore a bare minimum at home. They wore (at home) smocks of fine material or *bajus.*

The Portuguese were attracted by the wealth of the upper class Christians. A document available at Torre do Tombo states that in the middle of the seventeenth century the Municipal Council of Goa *(Senado)* requested the Portguese king to decree that " no *Brahmin* or *Chardo* who is rich or has property might marry his daughter to any one except to a Portuguese born in Portugal and such people must leave their property to their daughters"(ANTT:DRI-61:161) . However, M. N. Pearson in his *Western Coastal India* gives an impression that the document refers to Hindu Brahmin and Kshatryias (Pearson 1981:96-97). The motive behind this move was to increase the wealth of the Portuguese in Goa from dowries and legacies that these girls would bring. Besides once married these Goan women and children would embrace Christianity. Sons of such marriages would be prepared to join the army (Pearson 1981). The measures would also help the Portuguese to establish a large 'white colony'.

Non-Christian women who were more traditional than Christian native women led a secluded life and rarely ventured out except to attend a wedding or some religious festival accompanied by members of the family. On such occasions they wore festive clothes of expensive material and exquisitive jewellery. Hindu women wore a *sari* with a tight fitting *choli.* They adorned their hair with flowers. Muslim women of all classes wore *sari* with a *choli* or a loose dress and pants.

Hindu women had several duties to perform. Women had not only to look after their homes but also played an active role in religious ceremonies performed at home. Some of these ceremonies could only be performed by women. A Jesuit letter dated 1560 says " Brahmin women are reserved and virtuous, they are modest and submissive, they serve their husbands like slaves" (Costa 1965).

Women of the upper strata of all communities had plenty of leisure. They spent their time sitting at home, singing , playing musical instruments, embroidering, gossiping and looking out of windows. Some of these windows had shades through which the person who was inside could see a passerby and not the other way around. Christian women enjoyed equestrian games and folk plays which were staged in their compounds during festivals. They played cards or were entertained by their slaves who played music for their listening pleasure. Jugglers were hired to entertain them, sometimes those living in the city of Goa were taken for a boat cruise along the Mandovi river. There were some widows among the upper class Christians who managed the property of their dead husbands as *cabeça do casal.* In this position they had the authority to administer the share of the properties of their minor children. In early seventeenth century the Municipal Council of Goa was complaining to the Crown that many of these women deprived their children of their patrimony.

The outside needs of upper class women were taken care of by their husbands, numerous slaves or servants. The children of upper class Christian women were taken care by slaves who brought them up carelessly. Some women employed wet nurses for their babies.

Men were jealous of their wives. This is not surprising, taking into account some of their activities. Non-family members were not encouraged to come home. In case they happened to come in the absence of male members they were received by the slaves or servants.

The women of lower strata of all creeds carried out multiple roles of housewife, mother and even contributed to the family income. Women of lower strata were poor and could not afford any luxuries. They had little time for leisure except for annual festivals, marriages and religious ceremonies.

Women of this class wore *saris* in different styles with tight fitting *cholis.* Hindu married women drapped nine yards of *sari.* Christian women when visited the Church wore hol over the *sari* (Lopes Mendes 1886:i/ 48). The *Kunbi* women wore *saris (kapod)* in another style with or without *choli*. During the later period Christian women of this class too wore clothes in western style.

Monogamy was the rule, while polygamy was tolerated among upper class non-Christian men. Polygamy among non-Christians was recognized by *Usos e Costumes* with certain reservations. Monogamy was made compulsory for non-Christian in the second half of the sixteenth century but despite this law some men continued to be polygamous. Many of them also had concubines who belonged to the class of *bailadeiras.* Prevalence of such relationships did not as a rule lead to the break up of the legitimate marriages.

Hindu men were allowed to divorce their wives in case of adultery or take another, specially if she did not give birth to a son. However, women were not allowed to divorce their husbands. Boxer in his work *The Portuguese Seaborne Empire* writes that there was no excuse for adulterous woman, even if the husband was unfaithful. She was supposed to bear it patiently.

The mortality among girl-wives was high due to child birth as result of poor pre natal, post natal care and diet. Furthermore, since in Goa girls married early, this factor posed a risk at child birth. Women had a large number of children which also affected their health. Men of lower class were fond of alcohol and it was not unusual for them to beat their wives. Religion and tradition reinforced the oppression of women and permitted men to have exclusive rights of domination over her .

Linschoten was impressed with personal care of Goan women. In his words "By nature women were clean and neat. They had bath everyday and at times twice a day in the morning as well as in the evening. They washed when they eased themselves or had sexual relations. They used sweet smelling herbs, perfumes, frankincense and rubbed their bodies with sweet senders"(Linschoten,i). They were free of body odour. Women changed their clothes daily.

Sati–An Ancient Practice

Afonso de Albuquerque when conquered Goa had promised to respect local customs and adopted a policy of non-interference in the religion of the Hindus. Despite this solemn promise soon after the conquest of our land he banned *sati.* Albuquerque appears to have been genuinely concerned in abolishing this custom. As a foreigner the custom was to him inexplicable and evil. However, the motive behind this ban has been questioned by some modern Indo-Portuguese scholars. They believed that the purpose of such ban was to marry these widows to the Portuguese soldiers.

In Goa as in rest of India, women were expected to remain faithful to their husbands even after their death. They had to die in the pyre of their husbands. Despite Albuquerque's ban, upper class women were encouraged to commit sati. Tome Pires in his *Suma Oriental* writes that "it was mostly the custom in this kingdom of Goa for every heathen wife to burn herself alive on the death of her husband". Further, he states that force was used among those who refused. Missionary reports and travellers accounts of the sixteenth century and even later period refer frequently to the prevalence of the custom in Goa.

A Jesuit account of 1548 reports that when a non-Christian died outside the island, it was a custom for the deceased relatives to ask the woman to commit *sati.* In case the woman agreed with the plans great celebration was held with food and local intoxicating drink known as *urraca.* The woman dressed in festive clothes and jewellery would be taken to the pyre to the accompaniment of music. As she danced around the pyre, her gold ornaments were removed. In case she was reluctant she was intoxicated with *opium* and *urraca.* After that she was dragged, pushed into the pit (DI,i:253) and burnt alive.

In 1555, the Brahmins succeeded officially in repealing the ban (ANTT:CGSO- IG:36/5/3). By 1559 the concession had ceased, some leading Hindus of Chorao were refused permission to take widows along with their dead husbands to be burnt in the main land. A royal decree of 1559 forbade the practice of sati. The decree was implemented by a Viceregal decree of 1560 which banned sati in city of Goa, Bardez and Salcete. Nevertheless, the custom continued in practice. Linschoten gives a description of the custom. Another traveller, the Italian Petro Della, Valle who visited Goa around 1623, remarked that many widows were burnt alive with the bodies of their husbands.

In case a woman refused to die with her husband she was abused and driven away from her home by the members of her husband's family. Since she was not financially independent she had no other alternative but to lead a life of vice. Women who did not commit *sati* lived in horrible conditions (Bernier 1927). Some women took refuge in the temple of Malsadevi at Mardol.

Bodki – A Hindu Widow

A missionary letter dated 1560 says that from the time Hindu wives were forbidden to be a *sati,* they lived a miserable life of a widow. Many of these women were still young (DI,vii: 391). The conditions of a Goan widow, specially the Hindu widow, will be discussed in Chapters 3 and 6 of this work. Petro Della Valle, comments "If the husband die the woman never marries more, were she so minded, nor could she find any of her own race who would take her, because she would be accounted as bad as infamous in desiring a second marriage". Further he continues "Widows who cannot marry again commit disorders in private especially with men of other nations and religion and with any they find, provided it be a secret".

The conditions of Christian widows were slightly better. Among the Christians widow remarriage was permitted but many Christian women specially the native ones did not remarry as this was not approved by the society. Besides, if she married again she would loose the right to her husband's property. Generally, she led a secluded life. She was expected to mourn for her dead husband for the rest of her life.

The World of Escravas

Slavery was not unknown in ancient India but the arrival of the Portuguese gave a new boost to it, and Goa's slave market in the sixteenth century provided abundant and wide variety of slaves (Souza, 1989). In this chapter we are concerned about the conditions of female slaves *(escravas)* in the early period of Portuguese rule in Goa.

As many travellers have noted, hordes of slaves of different races were available and sold in the city of Goa. Slaves were procured from different parts of India and other countries including Africa, Malaya, Indonesia, China and Japan. The black female slaves were irresistible. The *Negras de Guine* (African slaves) were in great demand for their beauty. The famous Portuguese epic writer Luis de Camoes wrote about *Barbara Escrava.* The charming Indian slaves with dark big eyes, smooth bronze skin and long black hair were also desired.

Rua Direita known also as *Rua de Leilao* in front of See Cathedral in the city of Goa was a scene of bustling slave trade. Slaves were auctioned and bartered here. Slaves were even sold at the door steps of the Cathedral and the Viceroy's palace. Many slaves were owned by the Government and made to work in the galleys. The State did not show much concern towards the poor slaves. The Portuguese invested nearly a million *cruzados* only in the slaves they had acquired from Japan in the last quarter of the sixteenth century. Jesuit missionaries were involved in slave trade too. These missionaries made profitable investments in the slave trade. Slaves were bought at times in return for foodgrains, arms and ammunitions.

Slaves were owned mainly by the Portuguese and natives. Non-Christian natives were not permitted to own slaves. The ban was not really observed in practice (HAG:Ms.9529- LFC:187).

The role of slaves in Goan society has been debated. Female slaves were involved in all kinds of occupations, mainly household work, embroidery, preparation of confectionaries and dry fruits.They distributed water, sold small wares, vegetables and other commodities. Men often bought their wares attracted by their good looks. They tried to befriend these women with ulterior motives. Profits earned from their work had to be handed over to their masters. At times they were threatened with dire punishment by their masters to bring a certain amount everyday. Those who were unable to do so would offer their services to any man. Some slave women had knowledge of medicinal plants as for instance the slave of the renowned Portuguese physician Garcia D'Orta.

Fidalgos had a large number of slaves in their houses to cater to their needs. This was not only the case in Goa but also in the Provincias de Norte as well as in Lisbon (Figueiredo-Correia Afonso 1933). Female slaves were taken to Lisbon in home bound ships contrary to the ban imposed by D. Manuel, the ruler of Portugal (Boxer 1990: 234-235). The very fact that the ban was repeated later shows that it was not observed.

An early seventeenth century estimate indicates that each *casado* household had around ten slaves in Goa (Subrahmanyam 1993). In the seventeenth century a Mulato blacksmith at Goa was alleged to own 26 slave women. Rich ladies sometimes owned 300 slaves. Female slaves were accessible to the lust of their masters. The use of female slaves as concubines was frequent in the Sixteenth and seventeenth centuries. Slave owners prostituted their female slaves for the benefit of the masters. The profits brought home by the female slaves were used by the masters to maintain themselves. Viceroy Conde de Redondo forbade shipmasters and others from taking slave women on board of ships (APO, vi:1153).

Female slaves accompanied their *senhoras* to the Church. This gave them opportunity to meet their lovers. Often they would leave their *senhoras* at the Church and disappear to meet their lover nearby. We know of instances when female slaves robbed their *senhores* and *senhoras* in order to support their men. These female slaves were proud to have white men as their lovers. Any child born from such relationship was proudly displayed. When female slaves had a child from a free man she had the option to give the child to him and free the child from slavery. However, female slaves were rarely willing to part with their children.

Slaves were ill treated by their masters and when they fell ill thrown out of the house. There are several reports of cruelties inflicted against the female and male slaves by slave-owners. These abuses against the slaves are discussed in detail elsewhere in this work. The Church Provincial Council tried to check cruelties against the poor slaves but the State did not introduce any measure to improve their conditions. The mortality rate among the slaves was high.

Goan women in the first century of the Portuguese rule in India both benefited and suffered. *Sati* was abolished in Estado da India. Decrees were issued by the State and the Church to encourage widow remarriages. They acquired some rights such as property rights. At the same time many of them suffered due to religious persecution. Attempts were made to ban the Hindu practices. Certain reforms introduced during this period alienated Goan women from their existing culture.

3

GOAN WOMEN AS REFLECTED IN THEIR CUSTOMS AND FOLK TRADITIONS

The preceding chapter focussed on early Portuguese influences on the status of women. This chapter is concerned with customs and traditions in Goan society as they relate to women. Customs and traditions influenced the life of women in Goa both in a positive and negative way. Women were controlled through customs and traditions. Some of these customs gives us an indication on how men and society view women. Many of these customs have emerged from the demands of a male dominated society and the socio-economic conditions of Goa. These customs serve as indices of women's backwardness, prejudices against them, low opinion about women's capabilities and complete absence of women in decision-making. On the other hand the customs and traditions show the importance of women in various traditional roles – mother, housewife and in matters of religion.

Proverbs are used in this chapter. Proverbs that have been transmitted to us from generation to generation. Proverbs and sayings are important part of the Goan folklore. They reflect the attitude of the people and the entire culture. The Konkani language, the mother tongue of the Goans, has a rich legacy of proverbs known as *oparyo* (idioms) or *mhunnyo* (profound sayings). There are more than hundred proverbs about Goan woman.

A great deal of information in this chapter comes from oral sources. I have interviewed women from various communities and strata of the Goan society--Hindu, Christian and Muslim. The majority of the women I have interviewed were born and brought during the last fifty years of the period under study. Many of the customs are still being followed in Goa. I have participated in some of these customs for the purpose of this work.

Births, marriages and deaths were expensive affairs. Sums beyond their means were spent on such occasions on dowries, food, clothing, ornaments and entertainment. Celebrations at birth, marriages and religious festivals provided a welcome relief to women from the monotony of their lives. They provided opportunity to move out of the house, meet people and disseminate information.

As in rest of India, the birth of girls was not always welcomed. There was marked preference for boys over the girls for reasons discussed earlier in this work, specially in non-Christian communities. Prayers, fasts and rituals were performed and wows were made for the birth of boys. Pilgrimages were undertaken for this purpose, many times even across the border to Gokhand, Kashi, Pandarpur, Tirupati, Banaras and Kanpur. The Christians prayed to various Saints including their patron St. Francis Xavier and visited religious places. This marked preference for boys reflects the dominant social ethos. The birth of the son was welcomed with great rejoicing while the birth of a girl was often met with complete silence. Soon after the delivery the birth was announced with the beating of a copper vessel.(Bragança Pereira 1940, ii:271). In the later period birth of boys was announced with firing of three packs of fire-crackers while those of the girl with two. The naming ceremony among Hindus and the baptism ceremony of Christians boys was celebrated on a large scale.

Nevertheless, despite all prayers and pilgrimages if a girl was born she was not done away with deliberately, as it happened elsewhere in India among certain communities. Apparently, better care was provided for the boys, who often survived diseases. Until the present century there was favourable male sex ratio. Pronounced preference for sons led to poorer feeding and neglect of daughters (Silva Gracias 1994). Girls were breast fed for shorter period than the boys. Boys were given supplementary food earlier and on the whole were better fed. Male children were provided better medical care too. Boys were considered an asset. The following proverb can be cited as an example:

Cheddo zaloleak ani madd lailoleak bhed na. (There is no difference between the birth of a boy and planting of a coconut tree).

The son and coconut tree were considered profitable as they brought income to the family. The male child supplemented the family income through his wages and dowry that eventually brought when he married. The son stayed with his parents and looked after them in old age, while daughters when they married left their parents.

A girl's first menstruation was celebrated publicly by Hindus. The occasion was celebrated with a big dinner by some, while others distributed sugar and confectioneries to members of the family and friends (ANTT:CGSO-IG 36/23). This was a happy occasion, because it meant that the girl was now a woman; and among the non-Christians she was now ready to go to the home of her husband. As pointed out earlier, Hindu girls were married at the age of seven or eight in the early period of this study. The fact that the custom of celebrating the first menstrual period continued until a few decades ago, points out that the ban issued in 1736 by the Goa Inquisition was not strictly implemented.

Menstruation was an occasion for awe and fear. During her menstrual cycle, the Hindu woman remained segregated from rest of the family. She was considered ritually unclean for a period of five to seven days. Menstruation was viewed as polluting and the activities of women were severely restricted. Particularly taboo were cooking and any kind of religious practices. She was not allowed to touch her belongings and stayed in a separate room during those days. Even the food to be eaten by her was left at a distance and served in separate vessels kept for the purpose. Although it was very unhygienic, a woman was not allowed a bath until her menstrual cycle came to an end. At the end of her menstrual cycle she took a ritual cleansing bath before resuming normal activity. It is possible that the practice was introduced to give a woman some rest from kitchen work and religious practices in those stressful days. A Hindu woman in the past had to prepare for and perform several rituals.

Christian woman of lower class also followed some of kind of restriction during this time. They considered themselves impure and for this reason they did not receive the Holy Eucharist during this period. They too did not bathe until the menstrual cycle was over.

During menstruation Muslim women did not follow all the above restrictions, but they refrained from praying or touching the holy Koran. They were permitted to prey after they had a complete bath between fifth to seventh day. Muslim women had to perform some other cleansing rituals too.

Amchi, atam tumchi (She was ours, now she is yours) – Customs and Traditions at the time of Marriage

Numerous customs and rituals were observed at the time of marriage. Some of these customs differed from one community to other, but there were many common ones. Hindus when converted to Christianity and Islam continued to follow their earlier customs.

Girls in Goa were married very early. Among the Hindus the marriage was consummated sixteenth days after the girl reached puberty which was normally around twelve, hence the proverb:

Bara, chol ghovache ghora
(You are twelve, go to the house of your husband)

This custom was followed usually by non-Christians. Among the Ranes marriages were held at slightly higher age. Christian girls were also married early. However, the age of marriage was slightly higher.

Hindu girls rarely remained unmarried by choice. In this community an unmarried daughter after puberty was an embarrassment to the family, so the family tried to arrange a marriage for the daughter at any cost, before she reached puberty. *Vadhalem chedum modlolya gharak* (a grown up daughter in the house is a disgrace). Besides, it was believed that a woman has to be a mother in order to be fulfilled.

Customs and traditions at the time of marriage differed according to the social status, caste and the community to which the girl belonged. Marriage was a long process. In Goa as in other parts of India marriages were arranged by parents, relatives or a middle person known as *raibari*. The girl being young and submissive had no say in the choice of her partner, neither the opportunity to know her future husband before marriage. The feelings and taste of the girls were not considered. During the later period of colonial rule, Christian brides had sometimes the opportunity of talking to their grooms on a few occasions. It was said that:

Aplya nasiban ghov khavuntço
(A woman must accept a husband, fate has ordained for her).

Another proverb that shows that the couple had no choice in selecting the marriage partner is shown in this proverb:

Bail mevlea mhos, patkan ailam sos (You got a wife like she buffalo,one must suffer the consequence of ones sins). The woman was probably ugly like the buffalo. In Goa, even today large number of marriages are still arranged but the couples have ample opportunities to know each other before marriage.

This does not mean that girls did not fall in love and get married during the period under review, but it was an exception rather than the rule and that too in certain communities and classes. For instance, the *Mando Sorgu nitoli Go Nirmollu* is about a Christian *sudra* (lower class) girl who marries a Christian Brahmin (higher class) boy. The girl was not only of lower class but ugly and plain. Such matches were not approved of by the society. Normally, marriages were arranged after enquiries were made about the girl's character, caste and the economic position of the groom's family. Often the caste was the main concern. Gips in his work "Jacob e Dulce" describes the prolonged negotiations about the dowry and other matters among the middle class Goan Christians (Costa 1907: 19-22). In this class as well as in the upper class Christian families, ability to play a musical instrument such as a piano or the violin was merely one more accomplishment to claim during marriage negotiations, even though some of these girls had no inclination for music. Inter community marriages were rare particularly among the upper strata.

Girls were judged by the character of their mothers. A popular proverb maintained: *Avoi polleun dhuv vhor, dudh polleun mhos vhor.* (Note the mother's character and choose a bride, similarly buy the buffalo on checking the yield of its milk).

Girls from families with hereditary diseases, especially mental illnesses, leprosy and tuberculosis found it difficult to get husbands. In those days T.B and leprosys were considered highly contagious, besides they were then incurable.

The reputation of the girl was an important consideration, that was the reason why the parents guarded their daughters and got them married early. Girls were expected to be chaste at the time of marriage. They were not allowed to talk to men outside the family, neither were they allowed to go out unchaperoned.

In addition to moral qualities of the girl, the complexion too was important. Fair complexioned girls were in great demand. Fair was considered by many, as beautiful, while dark complexion was considered ugly. Two proverbs are cited here as examples: *Kali bail ghovachi, ghori bail desachi* (The ugly wife remains faithful due to lack of temptation while a fair complexioned one belongs to the public). It also refers to the temptation a fair complexioned woman excites in men. There is another similar proverb : *Kalem Devak barem, gorem ghovak barem* (God loves the dark one and the husband loves the beautiful one). Everything points to the fact that beauty is synonymous with "fair" here. The fair one had all the advantages. Since it was difficult to arrange husband for a dark complexioned girl some of these among the Christians remained unmarried, while others joined the convent to become a nun.

It was believed that a fair looking woman could get out of many problems and people were blind to her faults.

Ieki gori beastor khoddi chori (Let a woman be fair, this will hide seventy two blemishes). There is another proverb concerning fair looking woman: *Zachi bail gori to nidta aple gharini, zachi bail kali to vharta paynt zali.* (The one who has fair wife stays at home, the husband of dark looking wife casts his nets elsewhere). A good looking wife keeps her husband interested and happy at home, whereas the husband of dark woman finds it more pleasant to cast his net and trap his catch elsewhere rather have uninteresting time at home. It is said that the husband of good looking wife stays at home since he finds no pleasure outside but with his wife. It also could mean that the husband of a good looking wife need not stray.

Parents were advised to marry the daughter in a superior family and to bring a girl for a daughter-in-law from a lower economic status as can be deducted from the following proverb:

Aplem vorteak duinchem ani khalteak haddchem

So that their daughter could live well and improve her social position. The idea was not to lower the status of the daughter, at the same time they were advised to bring a daughter-in-law of lower class because such girls would be submissive to the rich in laws and also improve her conditions.

Mothers were anxious to get rid of their daughters in marriage regardless of the age and health of the groom. At times even an old man would do as long as he was rich. The dowry demands of such groom were small this can be gathered from : *Pantçam asurpiyantco ghovlo, kitloso ge, may, tagtalo.* (Husband worth five xerafins, mother, how long will he last).

—*Naka ge, may, Saxthiço-ghav.* (Mother, I do not want a husband from Salcete). This proverb was popular in Bardez (north Goa). Girls from Bardez would sometimes beg their mothers not to arrange husbands from Salcete (south Goa). These girls were probably reluctant to marry in Salcete because of distance, specially at the time when means of transport and communication were poor. It was believed also that marriages between men and women of these two talukas were not happy ones. Men from Salcete did not have a high opinion of girls from Bardez.

It was not easy to arrange a match for a daughter. Therefore, it was said that those who had daughters did not walk tall (*Chedvankarachi nan sadantç khalti*). They had the heavy responsibility of getting their daughters married. There were several obstacles that the parents had to face.

Marriages were expensive affairs sums beyond the individual's means were spent on such occasions; on dowries, food, clothing, furniture, ornaments, entertainment and gifts to the couple and members of the family. An *alvara* dated 1681 banned excessive expenditure on marriages but the practice continued. Another *alvara* 1729, decreed that the Portuguese and the native Christians could not invite relatives of third degree (Lopes Mendes 1989:38). The parents had to provide heavy dowry for their daughters and meet other demands. This is reflected in the following proverbs: *Eka lagnak bara vighnam* (For one wedding dozen hurdles).

Eka chedvak kazar karunk bara zutim zharaunk zay, (To get a daughter married you have to wear out several pairs of slippers). Slippers were and still are the common footwear of the Goans. Often they took the proposal (marriage) to several likely young men, before one accepted.

Chedvachya ghovak dilem itley thodem (It is not enough, however, much you may give to the husband of a daughter). This refers to ever increasing dowry demands of the groom who was not satisfied with what he received. The dowry given to the daughter depended on the economic conditions of the parents and demands made by the groom's side. Often debts were incurred to get the daughters married. Dowry demands at times led to conflicts among the families. There are cases when the girls failed to bring the dowry that was demanded, they were harassed and even tortured by the husband and in-laws. It is because of dowry demands that a daughter was considered a burden to the family as is aptly said in the following proverb: *Kazar Karche adim chedum zad, kazar Kartotç god* (The daughter is a burden before marriage, after marriage she is a pleasure).

Due to preference for sons and the fact that the parents had to spend large sums at the time of the marriage, parents did not show great enthusiasm at the daughter's marriage.

Baie-Kazar, sante-chitt
(Marriage of a daughter, invitation in the bazaar).

For the marriage of the son invitations were personally given at the house. The proverb indicates that the parents did not show the same enthusiasm at the marriage of daughters.

Lagnacha Velar–Customs at a Hindu marriage

Among the Hindus, the father of the girl or a close relative took the proposal of the girl to the boy. Wedding plans were finalized only if the horoscope of the bride and the groom matched and dowry demands were accepted by both parties. Horoscopes were matched for compatibility by a priest known as *bhat*. He had a chart with a number of qualities. At least eighteen of these qualities had to match in order to finalize the marriage plans. In case the horoscopes of the couple matched, then male members of the family would go to the temple for *Prassada* that was to receive the consent and blessings of the God. This was more a formality and some families asked the *Prassada* before taking the proposal to the boy.

A Hindu girl could marry the son of maternal uncle. This combination was encouraged and even expected by the parents. Maternal uncle was given great respect and played an important role at the time of the marriage of his niece. First preference was given to his son. In such case the girl did not have to make too many adjustments in the family but there were other risks involved which were not considered at the time of marriage. This combination was also not uncommon among the Christians, although not always encouraged specially by the Church because of the genetic risks involved in marrying close relatives.

A day before the wedding, the family of the girl sent her trousseau and other things to the house of the groom. Among the upper classes, girls were given dowry in cash and kind. Dowry in kind consisted of copper vessels, silver vessels to be used for religious ceremonies, clothes, needle work, jewellery, furniture and even animals. Traditional jewellery presented to a daughter of the upper strata consisted among other things of four fat bangles (*ghont*), two flat bangles known as *Patli*, four other bangles (*kankanam*), two bangles with intricate patterns (*todde*), *valle* arm bangles,*mangalsutra* — a necklace with black beads and pendant of gold — symbol of married woman. In addition of mangalsutra upper class brides were also presented with *moedanchem -gantlem, conthi, mohan-mal sorpoli*, *chandra-har*, *moniachi golsori* and other *mals*. Hair decorations consisted among others of intricate patterned *atti*, *gulab-ful* (rose), *xenvtem*, *chandli*, *salcam*, *surga-olessor*, *chanfeanchi-atti*, *kadkadim-fulam*, *pisollin*, *ghanti-sorpoli*, *bubdi*, *carabam*. A Hindu bride was also given the traditional earrings with seven stones. In the early period these earrings were set with pearls but in the present century they were set with diamonds stones. This was probably as result of improvement in the standard of living due to the growth of mining industry, emigration to other parts of India and greater contacts with the rest of the world. A bride of this class was also given a *notha*, *pili* (nosestud), and toe rings.

Women of lower strata, generally, were given dowry in kind. The gold given to a girl of this class was much less due to economic conditions. In addition, as with the upper classes gifts in gold were presented to the son-in-law at the time of marriage. Dowry was considered as a security for the girl in time of illness, unemployment of the husband or in case of his death.

The time and the day of the marriage was fixed for an auspicious day after consulting an astrologer and the *Bhat*. The Christians did not follow such practices but Christians did not marry in advent and Lenten season.

Sometime before the wedding, the bride was invited by her relatives for a *porcond* (farewell to maidenhood). On this occasion special food was cooked for her and she was presented with a gift.

Some days before the marriage, the Hindu bride had to go through a variety of rituals which prepared her for marriage and acquainted her with the family of the groom. Some of the important rituals are mentioned in this work.

It was a custom for the bride to wear a *chuddo* (glass bangles) along with five married ladies including her mother. The bangles were worn by the bride in uneven number, normally nine in one hand and seven in other. These bangles were of glass and green in colour — Green stood for hope and fertility. The bride wore these bangles to ensure long life for the husband, as glass was believed to have a special protective property. She was supposed to break them only when the husband died. The five other women participating in the ritual wore bangles of different colours. *Vovios* were sang during this ceremony.

This ritual followed by another ritual known as *Deucare* which was performed previous day of the màrriage. The ritual was held to seek the blessings of God so that the marriage ceremonies should go smoothly.

The *Datem* ceremony was the one in which the husking paddle was blessed. The husking paddle was used to grind all the spices and pulses, necessary for cooking meals for the entire period during which the marriage rituals took place. Five married women placed their hands on a husking-paddle prayed to gods and goddess for the success of the marriage rituals.

An interesting ceremony was performed on the previous day or at times just before the wedding ceremony. *Tel* is an auspicious ritual. The bride dressed normally a *sari* of yellow colour for this ritual. Women from the family of the groom visited the bride and brought along two containers, one with turmeric and the other one with oil. These ladies applied oil and turmeric with the help of two leaves from a mango tree on the forehead, neck, chest, shoulders arms and legs of the bride. This was done to prepare her for marriage. Oil was rubbed on the head of the bride. Turmeric and oil were believed to make the skin smooth besides turmeric is supposed to prevent infections. Oil on the head acts as a conditioner. When the *tel* ceremony was over, the bride was given a ceremonial bath near a banana tree in the compound of the house (Banana tree stands for fertility since it produces fruit every year). After the *tel* ritual the bride was not permitted to be out of the house until the wedding day. This is the reason why in the present day the ceremony is held few hours before the wedding. A similar ceremony was repeated at the groom's house by some members of the bride's family. Gifts were exchanged on this occasion. Parents were presented with gifts by relatives and friends.

The wedding was usually held at the house of the bride or at a temple which had the deity worshiped by the family of the bride. The wedding ceremony was conducted at the astrological auspicious hour by the *bhat*. As mentioned earlier the maternal uncle played an important role in the marriage ceremony. The bride wore a *sari* usually yellow in colour — the colour of the turmeric. The *sari* was the last gift of the family to an unmarried daughter. The main ceremony was known as *Kanyadan*. This was the moment when the family of the girl gave up their responsibility for the daughter and handed her over to the family of the groom.

Garlands were exchanged and rituals performed by the bride and the groom at the wedding ceremony. The bride was presented a *mangalsutra* (this was the sign that the woman was married) by the groom. She wore two *mangalsutras* on her wedding day–one given by her mother and other one presented by the husband. Soon after the main wedding ceremony, the bride changed her *sari* and wore a *sari* either red, green or peacock blue in colour. This *sari* was a gift to her from the family of the groom. Hindu married woman always wore a *sari* after her marriage. Before marriage she normally wore a *gagra* (long skirt) and a tight fitting *choli*. She had to wear a kumkum (a red spot) on her forehead and bangles on her arms.

At the fag end of the wedding ceremony the bride performed *Vainam dane*. A ceremony in which the bride distributed five coconuts to five married women for the good health of the groom. The major fear of a married woman was of becoming a widow, therefore, she always prayed for the good health of the husband. A coconut was used in this ceremony, as a coconut was considered an auspicious fruit. The above mentioned customs are still being followed in Goa, particularly among the upper classes.

Rituals did not end with the wedding ceremony. When the bride came for the first time to the house of her husband, several rituals were performed. It was a practice to place at the entrance of the house five mounds of rice and *podd* (measuring container). The bride was asked to kick the container and splash rice around as a sign of prosperity and good luck. This ritual was followed by a lamp ceremony. The mother-in-law handed over a lamp to the bride. The ceremony was performed to initiate the girl as a housewife. A member of the groom's family applied to her *Chandan* (sandalwood). Sandalwood was supposed to prevent infection and had a soothing effect.

The young bride was required to have a great deal of patience to deal with the mother-in-law and members of the joint family of various age group with whom she was going to live. The patience and stamina of the bride was tested during the *Kanjina* ritual. Five vessels (copper) were placed one on top of the other. The larger one on the base and the smaller ones on the top. Over these vessels a coconut and some mango leaves were placed. The bride had to remove carefully each vessel without making any noise and had to place them back in the same position. In one of the vessels, the family kept a gift for the bride usually a ring in gold.

The bride not only adopted her husband's surname but also it was custom to give her new name on the wedding day. Thus, she symbolically took a new identity after marriage. The groom was asked to write the new name of his bride on a plate. This name was selected by the parents of the groom.

A Hindu married woman had to perform *vratas* during the life time of her husband, for his good health and long life. A Hindu man did not perform any rituals for the good health of the wife. Every morning married woman had a bath and prayed to Tulsi (Ocimum Basilicum). Tulsi is a plant that Goan Hindus plant in front of their house or in their courtyards. They believe that Lord Vishnu resides in the roots of this plant. The plant has medicinal value too. It was used to cure cough and fevers including malarial fevers (Silva Gracias, 1994). A Hindu woman worshiped Tulsi by placing turmeric and flowers. *Tulsi* was worshiped for the good health of the family.

The wife had to be submissive to the husband. She had to walk behind the husband as a sign of respect and wait on him at the dinner table. Therefore, she did not sit with the husband and other male elders of the family during the meals. The wife was not permitted to call her husband by his name. When referring to him she used the term *amcho* (ours), *amguele*, *te*, my son's father, the father of so and so, my lord and in case he was a man with a professional course such as doctor, engineer or a professor she would refer to him by that title. This was a sign of respect as usually the husband was much older than the wife. Although today many women of this community are highly educated, still some of them do not call their husbands by their names.

Obligations of the Parents of Married Daughter

The parents of the Hindu married girls had to perform rituals and observe several traditions throughout their life. Just before the first monsoons, the parents of the married girl sent to her house *porment* (provisions). In Goa there was scarcity of certain food commodities during the rainy season. They had to be procured well in advance before the monsoons. Provisions sent to the daughter's house consisted of pickles, condiments, *papads*, dry fish, pulses, *vadayo* (made of rice and ash pumpkin) sweets including mango jam and other requirements. It was also a custom to present the son-in-law with an umbrella for the rains. This was one of the ways of earning the good will of the in laws.

During the first monsoons after the marriage, normally in the month of July, the daughter was brought home to the house of her parents to spend a month with them. This was necessary since girls were married very early in life. They had a few opportunities to meet the parents, particularly if they lived far. These young girls often felt home sick and missed their families.

The daughter stayed a month in the house of her parents at the end of which a ceremony was performed known as *Ashadh Phulam*. Relatives and friends from both families were invited for this ceremony. The family of the son-in-law distributed sweets to the guests. Among the upper classes the daughter-in-law was presented with a gift in gold and a *sari*. After this ceremony the young bride was taken back to the house of her husband.

It was a custom to send *ojins* with sweets and fruits to the married daughters on various occasions , particularly for important festivals such as Ganesh Chaturti and Diwali. Along with *ojins* other gifts were sent to the daughter and the son-in-law. The purpose of these gift was to maintain good relations with the in-laws. *Ojins* sent in the first year of marriage were large. *Ojins* contained packets of *xev, chivada, xencar padde*(savouries), sprouted pulses and variety of sweets like *laddus, neuroes, kapam and dud peddes*. Some of these sweets were distributed among the neighbours, relatives and family friends of the son-in-law. *Ojins* contained also fire-crackers, flowers and fruits both edible and non-edible. Some of the edible and non-edible fruits were used to decorate the place where idol of Lord Ganesh was placed. At the time of Ganesh Chaturti the son-in-law among the upper classes was gifted a *patt* (low sit) with decoration made of silver. The *patt* was used during the *pooja* to the Lord Ganesh. The son-in-law was presented also with ceremonial clothes to be worn during the *pooja* and a gold ornament.

At the time of Diwali the son-in-law was presented with a set of clothes, perfume and another gift in gold. In addition it was also a practice to give a soap for the ritual bath on this day. The purpose of these gifts was to maintain good relationship with the in-laws. Gifts in gold and in form of clothes were also sent to the married daughter.

Christian Wedding

Christian marriages too were arranged by members of the family, relatives or a *raibari*, but the proposal could come from either side. A number of customs and traditions were followed especially among the lower class. Some of these customs were Hindu customs which continued to be practiced by the Christians, despite the ban imposed on them by the State and the Holy Inquisition. In 1787 one Ana Afonso of Linhares (Sinquerim-Bardez) was accused by the Holy Inquisition of following non-Christian practices on the eve of her wedding (ANTT:CGSO- IG:36/23). Catharina Roiz of the same village was also accused of similar practices. Goan Christians at the time of the wedding, followed also some Portuguese customs that were either imposed on them or have come down as result of the mingling with the culture of the rulers.

Before finalizing the date of the wedding it was a custom to discuss the dowry demands with the groom and his parents. Dowry was commonly known as *dote* was a kind of security for the girl — material help to start her a new life. Some members of the bride's family accompanied by *raibari* visited the house of the groom to finalize the dowry demands. This visit was made with prior appointment and during the visit various members of the groom's family would be present. Questions about dowry were asked only when negotiation was in progress and there was enough interest on both sides. Prolonged negotiations took place about dowry and other matters regarding the marriage. Many times the question of dowry was responsible for terminating the negotiations. Among the educated families dowry was not always asked but it was expected. There were cases also were no dowry was considered but those were exception rather than the rule.

Dowry demands were put forward by the parents of the groom. Parents of the girl had to provide a long list of goods to get the daughter married. Debts were often incurred to meet these demands. At times these demands led to ill feelings between both sides. In the last decade of the Portuguese rule in Goa, the state helped economically backward girls particularly orphan girls by providing them dowries through *Montepio*.

Some days before the wedding, the bride was invited by her relatives and close friends for *porcond* — to spend the day with them. The bride was bathed with coconut milk to purify her, after which she was dressed in traditional clothes, garlanded and taken around visiting the neighbours of the host. A special lunch was prepared for her with different types of meat and vegetable dishes. The dessert consisted of *batica, folles, patollio, alva, jagradas and bebinca*. Some of these were sweets made of coconut, flour, jaggery and other ingredients. It varied from class to class and the place.

Banns were read in the Church before the wedding. Banns were formal announcement of intention to get married. These were read for three consecutive Sundays in the Church where the groom and the bride lived. The banns were read to unable the people to raise any objection (in case they had one) against the marriage. After the first bann was read the Christian bride of lower class wore a *chuddo*. Christian brides wore about 30 glass bangles (this custom is still followed in Goa)–fifteen bangles in each hand. The bangles were either green or of mixed colours.

Chuddo was worn at the house of maternal uncle. A bangleseller (*kakoncar*) was brought home for the purpose. During the ritual relatives and other women friends sang special songs seeking blessings and happiness for the bride. *Chuddo* of mixed colours was replaced by bangles red in colour after the marriage. Red was considered an auspicious colour which stood for passion and growth. A Christian married woman like her Hindu counterpart was expected to wear bangles during the life time of the husband.

A day or two before the wedding the bride and the groom were groomed for the coming wedding. A ceremony similar to *tel* was performed. This was known as *ros* (juice). The bride was smeared with turmeric paste, coconut milk, rice flour and leaves of abolim, to make the skin smooth, fair(ANTT:CGSO-IG:36/23)and prepare the bride for marriage. In 1736, the practice was baned by the Holy Inquisition.

Dennem or *dote* (dowry) was sent to the house of the groom a day before the wedding. The trousseau which varied from class to class consisted of clothes and jewellery. In the early period among the upper classes a *fator* set was also included in the jewellery. It was a custom to send a small image of baby Jesus in the trousseau. The bride was provided with some furniture. The main piece of furniture was a *armario* (wardrobe). Inscribed on the wardrobe was the name of the bride and the date of the marriage. Lower class brides were also given copper vessels. In the early period of this study, it was a practice to carry betel and areca nut along with the dowry. The practice was banned by the Holy Inquisition in 1736. Among the lower classes, dowry was given only in kind. The trousseau was displayed in the house of the bride before it was sent to the house of the groom. Crackers were fired on this occasion to announce the arrival of the *dote* to the house of the groom. Neighbours and friends were invited to have a look at the trousseau.

On this occasion the family of the bride sent to the house of the groom a *Ojem* (basket) with fruits such as bananas variety of sweets mainly *bolos* (cakes made of wheat, coconut and jagegry) *doce*–a sweet made of gram flour, sugar and coconut. The number of *Ojins* (baskets) sent depended on the economic conditions of the bride's family, custom of the place and demands of the bridegroom's family. *Ojins* were sent soon after the engagement, a day before marriage, important festivals and after the first confinement. This basket of sweets had significance for both the families. It helped to earn the good will of the groom's family and ironed out any difficulty that a girl may encounter in adjusting to the new family. Besides, sweets were meant to convey the good news of the event to friends, neighbours and relatives. Sweets were distributed to relatives, neighbours and friends. Exchange of *saguates* at the time of weddings was banned by a decree issued by Holy Inquisition in 1736. (ANTT: CGSO-IG:36/23).

Brides from upper classes were given dowry in kind and cash. In the early period of this study brides were given only dowry in kind but in course of time dowry in cash was added. This was the root cause of conflicts between the two families. Girls who were given dowry in cash were often asked to give up their rights to the family property.

A few days before the marriage the *bikrem-jevonn* was held–a meal on the floor on big mats in the house of both the bride and the groom, for the poor of the village. Neighbours and friends living nearby were also invited to participate in the meal. Suitable verses known as *zotis* were sung on this occasion.

The bride was not allowed to see the groom a day before the marriage. It was feared that such a meeting would bring misfortune to the couple.

Christian brides in early period of the Portuguese rule married in *hol*. Some women of upper strata wore *Fota-kimao* after the Church ceremony. *Fota* was a *baju* worn for festive occasions. It was made of red velvet, damask or satin with black border and embroidered with gold thread. The accessories used along with *Fota* consisted of a variety of jewellery worn on head, ears, neck and arms. The classical *fator* set was a part of this apparel. The set consisted of green stone in the middle with two corals on either side held by double chains. Together with the *fator* set, the women wore a set with five intricate chains known as *contti* and other chains. On their arms they wore bangles such as *nille* with matching *carap* on the ears. They also wore a number of small chains from the ear to the head, combs made of gold, silver or tortoise shell and rings in every finger.

During the later period of Portuguese rule, majority of Christian women married in western style clothes, as result of Portuguese influence. They wore white gowns made of silk, lace, damask or satin—white was symbol of virginity and purity. The gown was a gift of the groom to the bride. The gown could be tailored either in the house of the groom or the bride. It was a practice to give the tailor a gift in cash soon after he started cutting the material to make the dress. When the dress was ready it was sent to the house of the groom.

On the wedding day the sister or sister-in-law of the groom or any other close female relative took the dress to the house of the bride, along with the accessories including in many instances jewellery presented by the groom to the bride. In Salcete among the upper classes, the groom presented to his bride a gold set–a necklace, earrings, bracelet and ring. The set was worn by the bride on her wedding day. Among the lower classes the parents of the bride gave to the daughter all the jewellery to be worn on the wedding day. The arrival of the wedding dress was announced with firing of crackers. Until the first four decades of the present century, bridal clothes were sent among the upper classes in a *machila* or *dolim*. This was the mode of transport used also to bring the bride to go to the Church. When the bride stayed within the walking distance from the Church, she arrived with her party under a colourful *sotri* (umbrella) red in colour, held over the head by a peasant woman who was generously tipped. Together with the wedding gown another dress was tailored. The dress known as *saddo* was to be worn by the bride of lower strata at home after the wedding. *Saddo* was red in colour and made usually of *chita.*

Before leaving for the Church, both the bride as well as the groom received blessings from the various members of the family. Blessings were given first by the parents, grandparents, siblings followed by other close elderly relatives and neighbours. It was a custom in the villages to sing special songs in Konkani known as *vovios*.(ANTT:CGSO-IG:36/23). *Vovios* were improvised songs sung in praise of the bridal couple, their parents, relatives and important guests. They were sung by women who were close relatives or friends of the couple.

Along with the blessings the bride and the groom were presented with gifts in cash by various members of the family, family friends and neighbours. The wedding was held at the place of the groom. The royal *alvara* of 1729 forbade dances for wedding during the lenten season.(ANTT:CGSO-IG:38/15).

Customs and Tradition at Nikha

As in other communities marriages among the Muslims too were arranged by parents, relatives or a *raibari*. The proposal for marriage was sent by the boy's family to the parents of the girl. The caste of the prospective groom and the bride was important factor to be considered. Muslims in Goa were divided in three groups based on religion: Sayed, Sheik and Khan. A boy of higher class could marry a girl of lower class but not vice-versa.

Unlike the other communities in Goa, Muslim girls were not provided dowry by their parents. Nevertheless, there was an exchange of gifts between both the parties. The groom had to give *Meher* to the bride either at the time of marriage or later in form of gold or cash. The *Meher* given by the groom was fixed by the girl's family. This was a kind of security for the wife since Muslim men could easily divorce the wife by pronouncing the word *talaq* three times for a period of time and in the presence of witness. The *Meher* was usually small since majority of Muslims in Goa were poor.

Muslim brides had to go through the *ros* ceremony too. A ritual equivalent to Hindu *tel* and Christian *ros*. *Mehendi* ceremony was also held two days before the wedding. It was compulsory for every bride to have their nose pierced before the marriage. Muslim brides married either in *sari* with *choli* or a dress worn over pants and a *dupatta.* The clothes and jewellery worn by the Muslim bride on her wedding day were presented to her by the groom. Marriage was performed at the house of the bride and the celebration lasted for 3-4 days.

Role of the Young Bride

Life was not easy for the young married girl at her new home. The girl had to adjust to her husband and various members of the family. Young couples in those days lived in a joint family. The wife had to be submissive and dependent on her husband. There are several proverbs projecting this aspect including:

Dadlo bayle adlo

(Probably this proverb refers to the creation of Adam before Eve. It is a proverb used by the Christians). Man being the dominating partner, it was not unusual for him (particularly among the poorer classes) to beat the wife. In fact, the man considered it his right to beat the wife. It was even encouraged by tradition as can be seen from following:

Ghovan baylek marlyar demand na

(In case the husband beat the wife she has no right to complain.)

Pavsan bhizlem ani ghovan marlem sarkem.

(Getting wet in the rain is same as being beaten by the husband). It is both natural and easily back to normal. It was believed that it left no permanent scars. The wife had no right to complain. She suffered in silence. If the wife was ever to show any protest–it was something looked askance at.

Generally, the husband was considered superior to the wife but there were times when the wife had the upper hand over the husband as can be seen from the following proverbs:

Dhakteli mogachi, pun ghovachem utar na sostali

(The little wife is loving, but she will not tolerate the domineering ways of the husband.) This saying shows surprise that the little woman is not tolerant of the husband's lapses. The male is flummaxed.

Ghova poros bail motti, musol gheun dhanvta fatthi

(The wife takes the upper hand, she runs after him with a pestel).

Although the husband was considered superior to the wife, the wife was expected to manage the affairs of the home as reflected in the proverb:

Ghovan zoddlen, baylen sambhallem, ghar tharlem

(The wife is the key of the house)

There are many instances when the wife being stronger than the husband would beat him during their fights, the husband used to feel ashamed and tried to hide this fact from the neighbours. He considered it an insult to his manhood:

Ghe go, ghe go

(Take it, take it),the husband would shout when he was being beaten by his wife to make the neighbours think that it was him who was beating the wife. *Go* means she in Konkani.

A married woman had to be submissive not only to the husband but to the various members of her husband's family:

Kazar zalo, dha zannanch pangik sam.

(One who marries is under the sway of many).

The daughter-in-law had to remain submissive to her mother-in-law – *Sunechi satya mayche khala.* (The daughter-in-law is under the sway of the mother-in-law).

The relationship between the daughter-in-law and the mother-in-law were not always cordial leading to jealousy and hatred. There are quite a few proverbs about the mother- in- law and daughter- in- law relationship. *Bailechi khoxi poili, kazar zauchi, dusri veggli sorchi, tisri bhurgem ball zaunchi*. (The desire of a woman is to get married first, then get separated from the mother-in-law and to have children).

It was common for a daughter-in-law and mother-in-law to disagree. Their fights have been compared to the one between a dog and a cat — *Mayu-sunechem jinem, zot sunya-mazrachem.*

Another proverb says that a dog is better than a daughter in law (*Sunem hoy, pun sun nay*) of course from mother-in-law's point of view.

Maincheo kornneo xinkear, sunecheo kornneo tinttear. (The acts of the mother-in-law are hidden in the kitchen sink, the defects of the daughter-in-law are published in the market). *Sunarddem, chamarddem, ani mharddem sarkem.*(The daughter-in-law, the shoe maker's wife and mahar's wife are the same.) The daughter-in-law in upper class family was equated sometimes by the mother-in-law to low caste women. This proverb was quoted when a mother-in-law ill treated the daughter-in-law and wanted to offend her.

There is another that compares the treatment given by the mother in law to her own daughter and to the daughter-in-law. *Dhuvek tel amasnao aniquilar a divalechi divalek* (Daughter's hair was oiled (groomed) from new moon to the full moon, while the hair of the daughter-in-law was oiled only on festive occasions.). The mother took better care of her daughter than her daughter- in- law. In Goa, it is a custom to use coconut oil for the hair as a conditioner and to keep it black.

The ill treatment given by the mother-in-law led the daughter-in-law to complain to her family and friends about her mother-in-law as can be seen from the following proverb :

Hadli sun kalle gharache gun. (The moment you get a daughter- in-law all the secrets of the husband's family are out). It was considered a blessing not to have a mother-in-law or a sister-in-law in the house:

Nonnond, na zav, susegad rav.

(You have no husband's sister, nor husband's brother's wife, live happily after) . This is said to a girl on her wedding day who has no in laws in the house.

Women, mainly the ones from lower strata had to do all the household work, take care of the husband and other members of the family. In addition, she had to collect wood for fuel, cowdung for manure and performed several tasks in the fields. Women of lower strata worked also as wet nurses, *daias*,(midwives) and *aias*,(nannies). Hence the following proverb:

Dublyach marum naye bail, giresthitço marum naye ghov.

(Dalgado 1922:67) (The wife of the poor should not die before him neither the husband of a rich woman).

The proverb speaks of problems created by such situation. Among the poor, the man would be helpless without the wife to cook, take care of his needs and help in performing several tasks. A rich woman who has always been pampered in the house would find it difficult to look after the family affairs and property.

Husbands were normally very demanding, specially at the times of illness, their expections of what a wife could do never seemed to satisfy them:

Ganv padlyar kadhumyeta, pun ghov padlyar kadhum nazo (It is easier to look after a village rather than a sick husband).

The fidelity of the wife was many times questioned, specially when the man worked away from home for long stretches of time. Goan Christians in the last two centuries of the Portugueas rule migrated in large number to Metropolitan cities of British India and to Africa. They returned home after a prolonged absence. They normally left behind their young wives. What happened to many of them is reflected in the following proverbs:

Ieka poteant dnt were: Ganesha.

(You cannot keep two swords in the same sheath. One wife cannot have two husbands).

Man zano pap, may zano lankratço bap

(The conscience knows the sin and the mother knows the father of the son) or *Kharkasa ghovatchi bail xindal* (The wife of a jealous man is immoral).

Ghovache pathir, miryam vati

(Pepper is ground on the back of the husband) It means that in the absence of the husband the wife commited many irregularities. When the husband turned his back the wife had a field day.

Traditions at the Time of Birth

A Konkani proverb says that the wife who has a husband is always pregnant (*Ghovachi bail, sadantc garbhest*). In Goa married women were pregnant during the great part of their lives. Child bearing was a difficult process in Goa as elsewhere in South-East Asia due to lack of medical facilities and hygiene before, during and after the delivery. This was responsible for high mortality rate among women in Goa. Antenatal care did not exist in Goa. Furthermore, most girls married early, before they completed their growth. Poor body built and stature were major cause of obstetric risks.

Women had large families, specially among the economically backward class. In healthy villages the average number of births to each marriage was 6 to 8 children and in unhealthy areas the average number of births to each marriage was 2 to 4 children. There were times when a woman would give birth between eleven to fourteenth children. Therefore, it was not surprising that she spent a great part of her life giving birth to children. It was considered her duty to have children.

Infant mortality is one of the factors that contributed to large families. Women had children as many as "God wills". However, they followed sometimes the natural methods. In Goa and the rest of India there was the widespread practice of extending breast feeding till the infant was 36 months old. This pracitce was reinforced by Hindu custom that required abstinence from or at least limitation of sexual intercourse during the period of lactation. Similar regulations existed at the time of religious festivals. Hindus were prohibited to have sexual relations on the anniversary day of the dead parents, nights previous to the anniversary day of the dead parents, in the day time, at sunset, midnight and during an eclipse. The poor health and nutritional conditions must have had a pronounced effect on fertility.

Several rituals and ceremonies were performed among the Goans and particularly among Hindu women before and after the delivery, mainly during the first pregnancy.

The pregnant woman was advised to refrain from strenous work from the time the pregnancy was confirmed. She was permitted only light work. Great care was taken to keep her segregated from all influences likely to distress her feelings. The duration of eclipse of the sun was for her a period of inactivity. This was meant to prevent any disfigurement to the child. She was not allowed to visit or see a dead body as it was believed it would bring her bad luck.

Great care was taken to see that the pregnant woman did not eat food that were regarded as possiblly harmful to the baby. She was given special delicacies. A major concern was to shield the expectant woman and her unborn child from malevolent magic and spirits. Therefore, she was encouraged to remain at home as much as possible.

In the fifth month of the first pregnancy a ceremony known as *Fulam* was performed among the Hindus. The expectant mother was dressed in a *sari* and *choli* green in colour and she also wore glass bangles of the same colour. Her head was covered with flowers and she was adorned with jewellery. Women relatives and friends were invited for this ceremony. Men did not attend the ceremony. The expectant mother was given a gift in gold by her in laws. After the ceremony, the girl was taken to the home of her parents for the delivery. It was custom among the Goan parents to take the daughter home well in advance for the first delivery. *Phulam* was again performed at the house of her parents. The pregnant woman among the upper classes was offered a gift in gold by her parents. The purpose was to keep the pregnant woman cheerful and happy. She would return to the home of her husband about two months after the delivery.

The Hindus followed another custom in the 6th month of the first pregnancy. This ceremony was known as *Againim*. In this ceremony gifts were exchanged. Gifts were offered to the son-in-law and the daughter-in-law.

Among the masses a *prima gravida* was bled in the sixth or seventh month of her pregnancy. Apparently, to avoid high blood pressure. This practice of bleeding weakened the pregnant woman.

Prayers and offerings were made for the safe delivery by close members of the family, normally by husband, mother,or mother-in-law. Hindus resorted to various rituals. Christians besides seeking help of their saints resorted also to *ritos gentilicos* – non-Christian rituals. (ANTT: CGSO-IG :33).

Deliveries during the major part of the colonial period in Goa were performed at home by a *dai* due to lack of hospital facilities. Even when hospitals were established in Old Conquests, majority of women preferred to have their deliveries at home. Probably, because they were not used to the idea of having a baby away from home and due to their economic conditons. In New Conquests lack of medical facilities, transport facilities and poverty prevented women in need to seek the help of trained doctors.

The *dai* had no formal training. It was a hereditary skill or lack of skill that was greatly responsible for high infant mortality. The *dai* had little knowledge of hygiene and even less of obstetric science. She was illiterate usually middle aged or old and her only qualification was her experience. Unlike other healers she was of low caste, because among Hindus everything associated with confinement and to an extent with pregnancy was considered unclean. *Dais* many times performed superstitious rites at the time of delivery (ANTT: CGSO -IG-33/19). For instance in 1785 *a dai* from Chorao was found guilty of practising superstitious rites during deliveries by the Holy Inquisition. The *dai* was paid in cash and kind. She was paid extra if the baby was a boy.

The room used for deliveries was dimly lit, ill ventilated and away from family quarters. The child birth among the Hindus was looked upon as unclean and the woman treated as an outcast. When the labour began the prospective mother was suddenly separated from others. Cleanliness in the room was considered out of place. Windows and doors were closed to prevent fresh air. Dirty clothes were used during the delivery.

Deliveries were performed either on a chamber pot or on two chairs placed in such a manner that they resembled a chamber pot. This practice was followed even fifty years ago (Silva Gracias 1994). The child was received in a *sup* (winnowing fan). The umbilical stump was covered with a paste made of pepper and bandaged with cloth. Through this bandage hot oil was poured daily on the navel.

To bring the mother's uterus to its original position, the mother was placed on a mat or bed. The *dai* would press the mother's stomach with the sole of her foot.At the same time she would try to raise the mother with her hands.

The penknife used to cut the umbilical cord was kept under a pillow of the child till the sixth day of the birth. Similar iron material was placed under mother's pillow to prevent misfortune to the mother and the child.

As already said earlier the birth of the son was welcomed with great rejoicing. A girl born after three boys was known as *tickli* and she was considered a bad omen, as it was believed she brought bad luck to her parents and her husband. A girl born after a *tickli* was known as *niclli*. She too was considered a bad omen as it was believed that she would cause untimely death in her husband's family. Therefore, it was difficult to arrange husbands for such girls.

Among the Hindus when a child was born as a thanksgiving, the head of the family offered coconut and sugar to the family deity and the parents. Relatives of the mother placed areca, betel and a coin near *Rui*. They removed a leaf from the tree and placed it on the forehead of the mother.

The mother of the baby was fed with a cake made of flour and jaggery in the first three days, probably to give her strength.

During the first six days after the delivery the new mother and the child were in an especially great state of pollution. This was because it was believed that after the delivery the woman bled nine months menstrual blood. Therefore, she was not allowed to have a complete bath during the first six days. She could have bath from the neck downwards. This was probably because she was weak to go out to have a bath near the well which was at the back of the house. In addition, it was believed that head bath during this time could be responsible for tetanus, convulsions, cold and other health problems. Some leaves were boiled in water to prevent infection. However, in some communities, head bath was permitted on the third day of the delivery.

A ceremonial ritual *sotvi* was observed on the sixth day after the birth of the child. The purpose was to drive away evil spirits, bring luck to the new born and to prevent tetanus. Seven types of vegetables cooked with coconut were distributed to seven houses. Flakes of garlic were tied around the wrist of the child. The family did not consume water from their house well. The whole family kept vigil on the night of the fifth and sixth day. They spent the night singing and playing while they waited the visit of Dame Luck and Dame Fortune. It was believed that they visited the new child on this night. For this reason, the room of the child was rearranged. Close to the mother a mound of rice was arranged, and a vessel with cereal placed over it. The vessel was closed with a coconut and flowers of a shrub known as *potcoli* (Ixora Coccimia). The vessel represented goddess *Sotvi* and to her fruits and sacrifices were offered. These gifts were taken away by the *dai*. *Sotvi* was a custom followed even by Christians, despite repeated decrees both from the State and the Church against the custom.

As the family waited for the Dame Luck/Fortune, the area from the mother's bed to the front door was sprinkled with flakes of garlics, mustard seeds and grains. The natives believed that both Luck and Fortune competed with each other on this night to be the first to enter the room. Condiments were sprinkled to keep one of them busy collecting the grains while the other, usually Dame Luck, gave luck to the child and disappeared. Some people fumigated the house with gunpowdered and covered the child with black cloth, possibly to prevent tetanus and bad luck. In a joint family when this ceremony was performed, it was a tradition among the female relatives with children (who had not started teething) to stay away from the house for a period of 10 days. They stayed at the mother's place. This was followed so that the evil spirit that was repelled from the new mother did not enter the mouth of the child (who had no teeth to obstruct the entry).

For a period of ten days after the delivery the mother was isolated in a room. She was allowed to have only one woman for company. This practice was followed because the Hindus considered such women as polluting and also probably to prevent infection to the woman.

First eleven days after the delivery were regarded impure and therefore a woman who delivered a child was banned from participating in religious ceremony. It was believed that if she participated in such ceremony she transferred her impurities to the family and community, leading to misfortune or disease.

Another interesting custom *Pancha-gavia* was performed on the eleventh day after the delivery among the Hindus. *Pancha* meaning five and *gavia* meaning cow. The five secretions and excretion of the cow duda (milk), lounim (butter), tac (cream of milk), chene (cowdung), and muta (urine) were mixed together and given to the mother of the new born child.

A tradition was followed even among cultured people to decorate the door of the house of the newly born child with *marvel* (Andropogan Annulatus). It was meant to drive away evil spirits. Possibly, it was an antiseptic.

On the 12th day the naming ceremony of the child was performed. The mother and other women of the family played an important role. The mother rocked the cradle on and off. Rice, coconut and a piece of cloth for a blouse was placed on the lap of a married woman. After this ritual was over, the same married woman would announce the name of the child.

A sweet made of rice, coconut and milk was prepared for the ceremony performed on 20th day after the delivery. The *dai* took seven spoons one at a time, and waived it over the head of the mother and the child. At the end of the ceremony a small quantity of this sweet was kept in the place where the mother had her bath during the first seven days. The mother and the child were given oil massage for the period of a month.

Finally, the postpartum pollution period ended about forty days after birth. The last vestige of ritual birth pollution was removed in a ceremonial bath in which seven types of flowers were boiled. After this ceremonial bath, the woman was ready to resume her normal life. According to the custom women were not permitted to go out of the house for forty days after the delivery. In spite of a episcopal decree of 1784, Christian women continued to follow the practice. The custom was also followed by the Jews. The episcopal decree of 1784 advised Parish priest to convince such women to go to the Church before forty days. On the fortieth day Christian mother and the child visited the Church. Women had to bath near a well for two months after delivery.

Failing to conceive was regarded as a feminine defect. At times such wife was replaced among the non-Christians. Bareness was sometimes seen as a punishment for sins committed in a past life. Husbands were generally not blamed.In the early centuries of this period some Hindu women of upper strata in order to be able to conceive went around the pipal tree and those of lower strata danced the *fugadi*. They resorted also to various other superstitious rites to conceive (ANTT: CGSO-IG: 33). The glance of a barren woman was feared as it was assumed that she might bring evil to other people's children.

Hindu Women and Major Festivals

Religion played an important role on the lives of Goan women of all communities. Unlike Christian and Muslim counterparts Hindu married women played a major and active role during the religious festivals. She was involved not only in cooking and preparing sweets but performed also rituals. Some of these rituals were restricted to and conducted by women. In Goa, the Hindus celebrated a number of festivals, among these the most important were: Ganesh Chaturthi which in Konkani language is known as *Chovoth*, Diwali, and *Guddi Padva.*

Chovoth (Ganesh Chaturti)

Ganesh Chaturti is a festival celebrated in honour of Lord Ganesh, one of the sons of Lord Shiva and his wife Parvati. This festival was usually held in the month of August or September just before the harvest season.

A Hindu woman began preparations for this festival a month in advance with some religious rituals and fasts. This was the busiest season for Hindu women in Goa. It was her responsibility to prepare, well in advance sweets and other foodstuff which were offered to Lord Ganesh and were sent to married daughters of the family as well as to friends. The main traditional sweets prepared on this occasion are: *Neureos, laddus,chakli,chuda, sev and shanker padius.* As it was done in everyday life, the woman had to bathe before entering the kitchen to cook. She cooked a variety of vegeterian food without onion and garlic for the festival. Garlic and onions were not used in the food cooked for religious functions. The food before it was served to the family was offered to the deity.

Traditionally, women wore a new *sari,* preferably of silk for the occasion. Women of lower strata of the society danced the *fugddi* in front of the idol of Lord Ganesh.

Ganesh Chaturti was also a time for socializing for the women. Various members of family returned to their ancestral home during this season from different places. Women exchanged news and compared notes. In the evening they visited their neighbours and relatives living closeby and payed homage to their Lord Ganesh.

The festival was not only for socializing and cooking for women — it was a time for renewal of their loyalty to their husbands through rituals. The most important ceremony performed by the housewife on this day was *Gauri Pooja*. This ritual was performed only by married women. Gauri is the other name of Parvati, the mother of Lord Ganesh. According to legend Parvati who was then in love with Shiva observed a fast to invoke the blessings of God to be able to marry Shiva. God granted her wish. Eventually, when Parvati married him, she fasted every year as thanksgiving for the gift of desired husband. *Gauri Pooja* was also performed to ask God good health for the husband.

Diwali–the Festival of Lights

Diwali, the festival of light was celebrated soon after harvest season. The festival was celebrated in the month of October or November depending upon the Hindu calendar. Lamps were lit all over the house and around — in front of the *tulsi* plant which occupied an important place in the Hindu household and in the cowshed (Hindus worship the cow). On this day, early in the morning the family had a ceremonial bath. The wife applied oil to the husband and male children to smoothen their skin. Possibly, because the festival was celebrated in the cold season when the skin was usually dry. This was a service that the wife performed to the men folk of the house on whom she was dependent. This was also her way to show her appreciation and affection for the husband. The oil had to be applied evenly to every part of the body as it was feared that any part that remained uncovered by oil may turn black, thus disfiguring the person.

The wife bathed the husband after massaging him with a paste known as *vatane* made of some tender seeds, coconut shavings and turmeric powder. The purpose was to make the body smooth and healthy. The water for this ceremonial bath was boiled in very large copper container, decorated with garlands of marigolds (flowers of the season), mango leaves and a biter gourd. After bathing the husband, the wife would bathe the male children. This was followed by prayers. For this festival women wore their best clothes (usually new) and jewellery.

It was a tradition for the wife to cook on this day five variety of puffed rice in addition to other dishes. These five dishes were first offered to God on a banana leaf. Hindus eat on banana leaf on religious occasions. This was followed by another ritual, that the wife performed for her husband. A plate containing incense, five different leaves, areka nut and money was waved over the husband. The husband presented the wife with a gift in gold or cash and clothes depending upon the socio-economic status of the family.

Practices on the Death of the Husband

The role of a married woman changed drastically the moment she became a widow. She would lose whatever status she enjoyed in the society. Therefore, many husbands remarked: *Bhieun choltam, bailechim kanknnam rakhtam* (I live cautiously, I take care of the bangles of my wife).

It was a custom among women of all communites to cry and shout when the husband died. Hindu women fasted during the period the corpse was in the house. Women of this community were not permitted to attend the funeral ceremony at the crematorium.

Christian women of lower classes wore their best coloured clothes and gold ornaments on the funeral day of the husband. This custom was probably followed because a Christian widow had to mourn the death of her husband by wearing black for the rest of her life.

Following the death of her husband, a Hindu widow was stripped off her jewellery and hair. A barber shaved her hair — she became a *Bodki* — *bodki* was a generic name for Hindu widow. The widow was completely disfigured not to attract the attention of other men. Tradition demanded that she should break her glass bangles, remove the *mangalsutra* and wear either red or white coloured *sari*. Several other restrictions were imposed on a Hindu widow. A *Bodki* was expected to live a simple secluded life–praying and fasting. A widow was forbidden from chewing betel. In some families she did work of a servant. The miseries of widowhood were such that a widow preferred often to die on the funeral pyre of her husband as relief against the cruel world.

Apart from her disfigurement and humiliation, the widow was looked upon with suspicion. Believed to posses malignant powers a *bodki* was considered unauspicious. Therefore, she was held responsible for all the misfortunes in the family and the place where she lived. Consequentely, she was banned from attending auspicious occasions — *Rand bail konxyant, ayav bail munxyant* (A widow in a corner, a married woman among the people). She was also not permitted to perform rituals.

Christian and Muslim women too broke their glass bangles. This was a Hindu custom practised by Christians and Muslims. It was a tradition among Christian widows not to wear jewellery and mainly earrings for the rest of their lives.

Saptapadi (taking of seven steps in marriage) must happen only once in a Hindu woman's life. Therefore, she did not remarry even though permitted by law. However, a man among the Hindus was entitled to remarry even during the life time of his wife in order to get him a son . Christian men quite often married after the death of their wives. For this reason, the pain caused by the death of the wife was compared to the pain caused by banging of the elbow, while the death of the husband was felt deeply specially because it left the wife in a pitful state. Goan men were discouraged from marrying widows as it was believed that they brought misfortune:

Randek ghov tenklo, tatço modlo donko

(The husband touched the wife who was earlier a widow and he broke his leg). This proverb was mainly used among the Christians,since Hindu widows were forbidden to remarry. Even among the Christians, the vestige of opinion that widows were unlucky lingered.

The major fear of a woman was to become a widow. Hindu married women performed complex rituals particularly *poojas* once or twice a week to secure good health and prosperity for their husbands as well as good health for their children. One does not find married men performing any such rituals for the good health of their wives.

When a woman died at the time of delivery or 10 days after the ceremony of *pancha gavia* several rituals were performed. These rituals were performed so that the woman did not change (transform) herself into a *Xetan*, who was likely to disturb the peace of the family. These rituals were barbaric. It consisted in cutting the veins of the upper and lower organ of the woman and fixing a nail of wood on the head and closing all openings in the body with wooden pieces. The veins and arteries were cut so that the woman did not return home, a nail was fixed *para nao aniquilar a alma* , they closed the opening so that xetan that was in the body did not move out.

Some Other Roles of Goan Women

Freiras

Hindu women rarely remained unmarried by choice. Some Christian women did not marry. They joined a religious congregation to become a nun or remained spinster for life. A woman who joined a convent renounced material life and took three fold vows of chastity, obedience and poverty. Young Goan women joined a religious congregation for several reasons. The most important factor was vocation to religion. Women who joined the convent where at times accused of doing so to improve their status. This applied to women of lower classes. Lack of dowry, unhappiness and rejection by the loved one were the other factors, Goan girls were accused for joining a convent. Goan Christian parents encouraged at least one daughter to join the convent. In some families it was a tradition and status symbol to have a nun in the family.

Beatas

Several factors were responsible for young Christian girls to remain spinsters at home for life. Lack of suitable partners, dowry problems, lack of good looks, physical defects and too much expectations on the part of the parents can be considered as some of the causes. In present century the emigration of men to far away countries could also have contributed for girls to remain spinsters. Certain hereditary diseases including mental diseases and the caste system also played a role. Girls who could not find husbands within their caste remained often unmarried.

Sometimes girls of upper strata were kept unmarried because the family liked to keep its wealth as intact as possible within the family. Furthermore, in the upper class Goan families normally only the eldest son married, the remaining sons were forced to remain unmarried and one or two were sent to the seminary to be trained as priests. Sons were influenced to remain bachelors not divide the family property.

Unmarried girls of upper and middle strata hardly had options. Most of them spent their time in Church activities — they felt the need to dedicate their feelings to someone. They dedicated themselves to religion — praying, conducting prayers for the faithful, cleaning and decorating the Church. Some of them prepared confectioneries to the priests. These women were known as *beatas*. At home they tried to dominate their brothers and their families and looked after the family properties.

Camponesas, Peixeiras and Criadas

Women supplemented the family income by working in the fields alongside with their husbands. Agriculture was the main occupation of the people in rural areas. Among the cultivators *camponesas* (female farm hand) provided seasonal labour and played a distinctive role in both production and distribution. There was seasonal emigration of Goan women from early twentieth century at the time of harvesting and early July. The harvesting of crops was given out to teams of seasonal workers on contracts. Seasonal emigrants did not cross the boundaries of Goa. They travelled around the villages in small groups, returning again to their home base after a span of few weeks to a whole season.

In coastal areas of Goa, women helped their male family members in fishing activities. These *nustemkans* or *peixeiras* as they were known sold fish at the *tinto* or went around selling fish from house to house. Some other women went around selling vegetables from house to house or at the market.

Criadas (domestic servants) normally lived in the houses of their employers. This was the most exploited class in the Goan society who had no fixed hours of work and spêcified tasks. They performed all kinds of tasks from cooking to carrying errands. At times they played the role of a nurse to the sick members of the family they worked, companion to the old and nannies to the children. Domestic help in Goa as in Portugal were poorly remunerated. The plight of Goan domestic help was worse if they happened to be employed in the house of their *batcar* (landlord). They were paid no salary in the house of the landlord but provided only with poor quality food and some clothes. The kitchen was the place were they slept on a thin mat. Provisions for the health care were unknown. The work done by *criadas* was normaly not appreciated.

Consequently, many *criadas* migrated to British India and particularly to Bombay to work for British and Parsi families. The service conditions in these places were much better than in Goa. The emigration of women of lower strata was responsible for scarcity of domestic help in Goa as early as 1930's.

Poskem

Goan families of upper and middle strata sometimes "adopted" a child. Adoption was permissible only to Hindus according to their *Codigo de Usos e Costumes*. Hindus could adopt a male child in case they had no issue, from among their relations. Christians were not permitted to adopt a child as per the general laws of the land to which they were subject yet they "adopted" children in Goa. Majority of adopted children were girls. Christians families adopted children for several reasons. At time the *adopted child* would be the illegitimate child of one of the family members.

Some families gave the adopted children the same treatment they would give to their natural children. Generally, the conditions of the adopted girls were not always good —they enjoyed no status in the society and were looked down upon. In most families adopted girls were made to work in the house as servants. They were loyal and dedicated to the family . They worked like slaves but rarely their work was rewarded suitably. *Poskems* received no salary for their work neither they had any right for the immovable properties of their adopted parents. Most of them were kept unmarried in the house of their adopted parents. They looked after their parents specially in their old age with great care and affection.

Bailadeiras de Goa

Bailadeiras were Hindu dancing girls who belonged to a class known in Goa as *kalavantam* (derived from *kala* meaning art). The Portuguese called them *bailadeiras.* They dedicated themselves to god. *Bailadeiras* danced and sang in the temples. On festive occasions they danced in public and in the houses of well known people including Portuguese officials. According to *Farol* of 1526 *bailadeiras* had to dance first in the house of most important *Gaoncar* of the village (HAG:RG-LV:1/155v).During the time of Gaspar Correia *bailadeiras* danced every Sunday at lunch and dinner time at the Terreiro do Sabaio overlooking the palace where the Viceroys of India lived until 1554.

Four groups of women performed several duties at the temple. They were : *Colvontas or kalavantam, Chedvans, Deulinas* and *Bandens.* In British India these women were known as *Devadasis.* In Goan society the generic name for such women was *naiquins.* The offsprings of *naiquins* were known as *cheduanle.*

They were initiated in the profession through a ceremony known as *Xens.* The girl was presented for the ceremony by an important person of the village. This man had the right to enter into a union with the girl after puberty.

The Xens ceremony was exactly like a marriage but with a difference. In this ceremony the girl was married to an object, a flower usually a *hibiscus* or another girl dressed as a man. It was a ceremony of initiation. The ceremony was also known as *atlaulim* which means caressing or touching with hands. This ceremony was banned by the State through a legislation issued on 31st July 1930 (LREI 1930:248).

Widows of the upper class joined the profession including pregnant widows when they were thrown out of their homes. Some women in this profession were those divorced or abandoned by their husbands.

Bailadeiras wore colourful saris when they performed their usual dance. These saris were either of brocade(*pitambor*) or silk with gold or silver border. Silk saris were imported from Belgaum, Chapur or Nagpur. The *cholis* were made out of velvet or satin and embroidered with gold thread. However, when they performed the *Peshwa dance,* they wore long dresses embroidered with sequins and loose pants. Jewellery was profusely used on hair, neck, arms, nose and ankles. Anklets (*paenzonnam*), toe rings and nose rings (*noth*) were their distinctive trade marks. *Bailadeiras* wore aromatic flowers such as *mogarins, zaios, champins and abolims* on their head. They ate a hash of spiced greens (*Xaky baji*), with vegetables such as *tendlim* and cucumbers as added savouries. They ate betle leaf and nut for breakfast and butter and ghee for lunch besides other normal food.

Socio-economic conditions forced *bailadeiras,* in course of time, to offer their services to temple priests and high class men. Some men of the latter class kept them as their mistresses and offered donations to the temples to which the girls were attached. Various accounts available reveal that the Portuguese too were fond of the dancing girls. In course of time the choice of men was no longer restricted except for *Harijans* (untouchables). *Bailadeiras* contributed to the upkeep of the temple. These women had different status from other prostitutes. At times the illegitimate daughters of Brahmins were handed over to these women and initiated in the profession.

Majority of *bailadeiras* lived in New Conquests, where many great temples were situated. According to the English traveller Richard Burton who visited Goa in mid nineteenth century, there were about 20 establishment in Seroda (Siroda-Ponda) with a total of fifty to sixty dancing girls.

At the turn of the nineteenth century *bailadeiras* began to migrate to British India to improve their standards of living. Majority of them settled in Bombay where they accumulated wealth. Some of them established permanent contacts with wealthy men like rich traders, nawabs, rajas and high ranking British officials. They remained their mistresses and had children from these unions. As for instance, the well known Batia Naiquini Calangutcar. She was a mistress of an Englishman Mister Jorge, a General in the British army by whom she had many children, with the condition that all these children would be the heirs of the said General with no rights to the property of the mother (OP,1906:3/339). She left her own property in Goa to her niece Caxy and various temples in north Goa. *Bailadeiras* were able to give their children education and better standards of living with the capital they acquired from their lovers.

The Census of 1910 reveals there were about eight hundred and fifty two *bailadeiras* in Goa. The highest number of *bailadeiras* were found at Ponda, followed by Pernem taluka. Ponda taluka had the highest number of temples. The Census of 1921 show that Goa had four hundred and five *bailadeiras*. The lowest number of *bailadeiras* were found at Marmugao taluka followed by Salcete taluka, probably because very few temples were situated in these areas.

When the ceremony of *Xens* was officially abolished in Goa, a number of *bailadeiras* left Goa and settled elsewhere in India. *Bailadeiras* knew to read and write in Marathi. A few could even recite Sanskrit *shlokas* (stanzas) Most of these women were good looking and hospitable. These ladies were not only fond of betel-nuts, alcoholic drinks but also liked to smoke. A large part of their earnings were invested in gold and pearl ornaments. The establishments were run by matrons who collected great deal of furniture, linen and clothes.

Bailadeiras have been the theme of poets and writers. These writers have focussed on the conditions of these women. The amorous life style of *bailadeiras* is depicted by various travellers who visited Goa. More details about *bailadeiras* are discussed later in this work. Women who danced in public were looked down upon by the society.*Bail natçli, Laz hogdayli* (A woman who danced in public lost her reputation). Men were not prepared to marry such women.

Daughters of *bailadeiras* also became *bailadeiras.* Illegitimate daughters of Brahmins when handed over to *bailadeira* were initiated in the profession soon after puberty.

Bavinas were girls dedicated to the temples by their parents at a young age. Such practice still exists elsewhere in India. These girls had to perform several duties in the temples such as cleaning the idols, carrying the earthern lamps and lighting them for worship. *Bavinas* did not dance in the temples. Germano Correia says that they did not involve themselves in prostitution and remained virgins throughout their life. However, some other available literature says that they too were traditionally connected to men of the Gawd Saraswat Brahman Community. Majority of the *Bavinas* lived in north of Goa.

Badens were not attached to the temples. They were the result of illicit affairs between the master and the servant. The conditions of these women were miserable. *Deulinas, Chedvans and Bandes* could not dance in the *Duila* (temples in Konkani). *Deulinas* usually lived on the outskirts of the *devalais* (temples), in their own homes from where they carried their trade. *Chedvans* could work in the temples but were not allowed to live in or around the temples (Germano Correia 1938: 77). The naiquins had different legal status from those of other prostitutes.

Solteiras

As we have pointed out earlier prostitution was wide spread in Goa and mainly in city of Goa. Men of all strata of the society, spent time with women of low moral character which included irresistible slaves as well as ladies of high society. During the later period, they were found also in the port area of Mormugao and around military camps. Several legislative measures were taken by the State and the Church to curb or control prostitution. These measures will be discussed in detail later in this work.

Socio-economic conditions of the times contributed to prostitution. Majority of people were poor. Women deserted by their husbands or their relatives were easy victims of the vice. Widows left destitute by their husbands often joined the trade. In the last century emigration of Goan men, particularly of married men, led some of their wives into prostitution.

Prostitutes were responsible for spreading venereal diseases (Silva Gracias 1994). The disease was known in Goa as *bailli pida* or *phirgi rog*. The disease is said to be brought from West Indies to Europe by the Spaniards and from Europe the disease was brought to Goa. It was disease which the people were not ashamed of. It was treated with *Pao de China (China root)*.

We have estimates for registered prostitutes in the twentieth century. According to the Census of 1900 there were about 1,119 registered prostitutes in Goa. The highest number, 397 lived at Ponda taluka, followed by Bardez which had about 109 prostitutes while Satari had the lowest number with just 15 prostitutes. It is possible that the number might have been higher as all of them did not register and carried clandestine trade. There are references to open flesh trade in the capital city around 1925. The table below shows the number of prostitutes in various talukas of Goa in 1931.

Talukas	*Number of Prostitutes*
Ilhas	119
Salcete	172
Bardez	186
Mormugao	44
Pernem	111
Sanquelim	147
Satari	44
Ponda	277
Sanguem	70
Quepem	74
Canacona	85

These were the registered ones. In 1934 the number of registered prostitutes was about 1,000 in Goa. In 1936 there were about 1,748 Hindu prostitutes, 141 Christians and 9 Muslims. Hindu prostitutes were in majority probably due to religious views on sex, no widow remarriages and institution of devadasis.

In the mid 1930's the authorities with the help of Police pressurized the prostitutes to undergo regular medical check up in some talukas of Goa. These women often avoided these checks either by going underground or getting a male friend to file a petition in the Municipality declaring that she was mistress of the petioner and not a prostitute. Prostitutes had to register themselves during this period either with the Municipality or with the Police.

A gradual increase in clandestine prostitution was noticed in the first fifty years of the twentieth century, particularly in Bardez and Salcete. Many men from these two talukas migrated to rest of India, Africa and other places leaving behind their young wives. Some of these men could not send regular remittances back home causing economic burden on the wives. Males, who migrated, had sometimes mistresses in the place where they worked, neglecting the wife back home.

During the same period there was also an steady emigration of Goan women to other parts of India in order to improve their socio-economic conditions. They migrated mainly to Bombay. Economically deprived women at times involved themselves in flesh trade in the *Kuds* where they stayed in Bombay. A committee was constituted in Bombay to study the conditions of Goan prostitutes in that State. The committee submitted its report in 1923, according to the report about 510 prostitutes born in Goa plus their 225 female dependents lived in Bombay. Germano Correia gives an estimate of 2,000 prostitutes of Goan origin in Bombay around 1931. In addition, there were over hundred brothel keepers of Goan origin. The estimate is based on registered ones. Majority of these women belonged to the class of *bailadeiras.*

A report sent by a Health Officer of Pernem states that in the third and fourth decade of the twentieth century majority of the prostitutes in that area were those who had spent their youth at Bombay in similar activities. While the Health Officer of Canacona — one of the poorest taluka situated in South Goa states that suicide cases among the prostitutes were not unusual during the same period. They got themselves drowned or swallowed a poisonous plant known as *vagacho danteo* which was very toxic.

Leisure

Women of the upper strata of society as stated earlier had plenty of leisure. The women of the lower strata of society hardly had free time. They worked hard from dawn to dusk. Since they worked along with men in the fields, they enjoyed greater freedom than women of upper strata. Life was monotonous. Women looked forward to festivals, fairs, weddings and other such occasions to relieve the monotony of their existence. The Hindus had their religious Chaturtis — Ganesh and Diwali and other festivals such as Haldi Kumkum held once a year when women visited each others homes. This festival was held in month of January. Small gifts were exchanged by women. The festival was celebrated by married women. They also attended *zatras* with male members of the family and visited fairs held on such occasions. These fairs gave girls and boys opportunity to see each other before marriage proposals were settled. Hindu women of some classes danced *fugree* to the beat of the *Ghumatta* through the night on certain occasions.

The Christians too, had their religious feasts with fairs outside the Church. Christmas was an important feast for women. They prepared a variety of sweets for this occasion such as *mandare, kormolam, neureus,dodol, alva, batica and bebinca.* Weddings gave women from all communities opportunity to meet and mix. Christian women of the upper strata from the end of nineteenth century onwards danced the Mando at weddings. Kunbi women (tribal) danced to the beat of *ghumatta* (drum). They participated in *Zagor* (gauddha theatre). During the *carnival* folk plays were staged in the villages.

How Goan Men View Some of Their Women

Until the last fifty years of the Portuguese rule in Goa majority of Goan women were not educated. Women were considered by some men to be foolish and lacking in intelligence. She was equated to an ass and other animals. Though women are important in the life of men. Yet men had low opinion of women's intellect. The following proverbs shows contempt for women's understanding :

Bail-munxyank dhompra sakal budh
(Woman wisdom is below the knee).
Saglyam baylank ordhya gadhvachear gnyan
(All women put together posses the intelligence of half an ass.)

Baylechem xahanepan touli kade
(Women's wisdom is near the kitchen).
Bayleche budhik bhullo, gharatço bhangastal kelo (The husband was bewitched with the advise of the wife and the house was in ruins.) Many women do not know to keep secrets.

Bailechi jibh bakdechi xampdi
(A woman's tongue wags like a snake's tail). The snak's tail is always moving.

Bailankoddem gutt sangum-naka, raiakodden fott uloum naka, chovganchem utor moddum naka (Do not confide your secret to a woman, do not tell lie to a king, do not go against the wishes of the majority.)

Bail dhavea paianchi vhann (The woman is left foot's sandal). Therefore not much importance was given to her–a doormat–to be used and tramped upon.

Certain habits among the women die hard. The following proverb describes the waspish behaviour of a woman, she is born with and she dies with it :

— *Chinch sukli azalear, tichi ambttan vochona*

(The tamarind may be dry but its acidity does not pass).

Some women were very fond of gossip and once they started talking they would forget the duties of serving meals to the husbands. The wife carried food to the husband when he was working in the field as shown in the proverb:

Gozalint gozali, porsant bail ghovak visorli

(The wife was lost in a group conversation, and forgot the husband in the field).

Migration of Goan Women

Emigration of Goan to other parts of India started in the early centuries of the Portuguese rule . Women migrated in the company of their families to neighbouring kingdoms to avoid being converted to the religion of the rulers. After this period the emigration of Goan women slowed down.

Goan women started again migrating in large numbers in the twentieth century, for different purposes. They migrated mainly in two directions–to Africa and British India. Goan women who migrated to Africa were the ones who went there to join their husbands or as brides to Goan men settled there–Goan men in Africa were involved in pioneering work in many fields including medicine. Women who migrated to Africa were Catholics and belonged to middle and upper strata of the society. Goan women in Africa did not settle there permanently, eventually they returned home to provide their children with western type of education and to imbibe in them Goan culture.

Majority of women who migrated to British India settled in Bombay. They were predominantly of lower strata of the society. These women were between the age group of 14 to 45 years and were generally unmarried or widows. They belonged to Christian and Hindu communities. In Bombay and other cities Goan women worked in offices, factories and as domestic help. Another group of women that migrated to British India were the *Bailadeiras*.

Majority of Goan women who migrated to British India worked in the houses of British and Parsi families. These women in Bombay were well known for their loyal and honest service. They were responsible in spreading the Konkani language, Christian doctrine and Goan culture among the children they helped to brought up.

4

STATE LEGISLATION ON WOMEN IN GOA

In the earlier chapters we have discussed the position of women before the Portuguese arrived in India, early influences of the colonial rule on the status of women and the customs and traditions concerning women. In the present chapter and the one that follows, the focus shifts to various legislation issued by the State and the Church. These legislation were issued to improve or control the activities of women throughout the Portuguese colonial period.

A considerable amount of legislation on women were enacted during the Portuguese rule in Goa. In the early centuries of the Portuguese rule in Goa, legislation such as property rights were granted to Christian women only. The position of Christian women before the law was the same as their counterparts in Portugal but the same could not be said about the non-Christian women in the early period. They were deprived, for instance, of property rights.

Majority of these legislation were not properly enforced or were ignored in the early centuries of the Portuguese rule in Goa. We find many of these legislation repeated from time to time. Legislation on women were difficult to enforce, due to the attitude of the society, particularly the attitude of men towards women. In a patriarchal society like ours, men believed, that woman should not enjoy certain rights. They found ways of not implementing some legislation, as for instance, the one that gave sons and daughters equal rights to their father's property, or the ones that discouraged *sati* and encouraged widow remarriages. The Government found it difficult to ban the activities of *bailadeiras* despite repeated legislation with heavy penalty, possibly because it suited the men to perpetuate these activities. At times the Government was also reluctant to enforce legislation on the people, so as to avoid hurting their feelings.

Some of these legislation were issued by the Portuguese Crown, while others were issued by the Viceroy of *Estado da India*. In the early period of the Portuguese rule, legislation were issued separately for Estado da India. These legislation, issued by the Portuguese rulers, helped to improve considerably the position of women, particularly the Christian ones, who were the first to benefit from the various laws.

The Portuguese Civil Code of 1867 was extended to the colonies in 1869. This Civil Code further improved the conditions of the Goan women, to begin with the position of the Christian women. The Code is uniform for all citizens, irrespective of creed, caste or sex, save in such cases as specifically stated. The Civil Code guaranteed equality of sexes with respect to property, while in conjugal life, the wife was expected to be obedient to the husband. The Civil Code contains laws, concerning the family, and safeguarded the interest of the widows and unmarried women and raised the age of marriage.

Although the Hindu inhabitants of the Old Conquests, were governed by the general laws of the land, their counterparts in the New Conquests, came under *Codigo dos Usos e Costumes*. The existence of two sets of codes for the Hindus created problems. Therefore, in 1880 the Government, after introducing necessary alterations, applied the *Codigo dos Usos e Costumes,* to the inhabitants of Old Conquests, as well to those of the New Conquests. However, Hindus had now the choice to opt out of the *Usos e Costumes,* and to seek justice under general Civil Code.

In 1910, Monarchy was abolished in Portugal and a Republic was set up. The constitutional change of 1910 brought about changes in the structure of the Civil Code of 1867. The Civil Code was liberalized. It gave women more freedom, and introduced alterations concerning laws on marriage, divorce and protection to children. It helped further, to improve the conditions of women in Portugal and her overseas colonies. Further changes were introduced in 1930's, and again when a *Concordat* was signed between the Portuguese Government and the Holy See at Rome. The Portuguese Civil Code is still in force in Goa although the Civil Code of 1867 has been replaced in Portugal.

This chapter has two sections. The first section is largely concerned with legislation enacted, to improve the conditions of women during the Portuguese colonial rule in Goa. The second section of the chapter deals with reforms introduced to provide women with education.

I. LEGISLATION ON WOMEN FROM THE SIXTEENTH TO TWENTIETH CENTURIES

The End of an Ancient Custom–*Sati*

One of the first reforms introduced by the Portuguese to improve the conditions of women in Goa was to end the practice of *sati*. *Sati* means virtous woman, in course of time the term was applied to mean the practice by which the woman died in the funeral pyre of her husband.

Albuquerque abolished this practice soon after the conquest of Goa (Commentarios, 1973:117). Those involved in encouraging this practice, inducing, or advising it, were liable to lose their professions and become slaves (CAA II). But the practice continued in Goa for a long time. In mid sixteenth century, the Hindus, who glorified *sati*, prevailed on the Governor, Dom Francisco Barreto, to officially lift the ban and permit women to commit *sati* on the pyre of their dead husbands (ANTT:CGSO-IG:36/5). Dom Francisco Barreto, who was new to Goa, succumbed to the pleas of the Brahmins and lifted the ban on *sati* in 1555. Many Christians including the Church authorities, protested against the move.

By 1559, *sati* was once again losing official support. In 1560 Portuguese India, had a new Viceroy, Dom Constantino de Bragança, who, on Royal advice, decided to revise the Viceregal decree of Dom Francisco Barreto. The revised decree of 1560, again forbade *sati* in the island of Goa and for the first time, in other parts of the Old Conquests (Bardez and Salcete). Persons involved in encouraging the practice would lose their property and liberty. Half of this property would go to the denouncer and the other half to the pious work of S. Tomas (HAG: Ms.9529-PFC:78v). Sati was abolished in the New Conquests as late as 1884.

Property Rights

After the abolition of *sati*, the next social problem, concerning women that attracted the attention of Portuguese rulers, was the miserable plight of the widows, particularly the Hindu widows who were not permitted to remarry.

Women in Goa, before the Portuguese conquest of the land, had no right to the family property. According to the laws of Manu, they had to be dependent, first on their fathers and then on their husbands. In case the husbands died, on their sons. This situation caused great hardships to widows and daughters.

In 1526 Afonso Mexia, the *Vedor de Fazenda* , issued a *Farol* (BNL-Farol dos usos e Costumes:128). Afonso de Albuquerque, conqueror of Goa, had promised to respect the customs and traditions of the native inhabitants of Goa. The *Farol* of 1526 protected the religion, customs and traditions of the Hindu inhabitants of Goa. Many of these customs and traditions were based on Dharmashastra. Nevertheless, the interests of the Hindu women were not protected. This *Farol,* among other things, recognized the right of men, as per the custom of the land, over their family property. On the death of the father, the property would go to the son, and from the son, to the grandson. Thus, the property would go to the male side of the family. Hindu widows and daughters were excluded from the family property, both movable and immovable (APO 1992,V:118-129). They were entitled only for maintenance. However, Hindu widows and eldest unmarried daughters of a *gauncar or a culachari* of comunidades de Ilhas, were entitled to *jonos,* in case the deceased died without a son (Xavier 1907:50). Christian widows and daughters had the right to the property of their husbands and fathers. Many times, fathers tried to deprive their daughters of their property rights. Generally, women had to depend on male members of the family.

Farol of 1526 was applicable to the inhabitants of the Portuguese territory in Goa and it underwent changes after the acquisition of *Novas Conquistas* . In case a man died without male heir, the property would go to the Portuguese Crown in a peculiar manner. The movable property of a person, who died without male heir, was auctioned to the highest bidder. The proceeds of this sale after paying the man's debt would go to the Crown. In case of immovable property, the first option of buying the property was offered to the close relative of the deceased who had to pay the price within five days. If he was unable to buy the same, it was auctioned to the highest bidder from among the village elders. The proceeds after clearing the debts of the deceased would go to the State. But this often did not happen because according to Hindu religion, polygamy and bigamy were recognized and a man could marry again if his wife failed to have a male child (Xavier 1861:4). Besides, according the *Usos e Costumes* of the land, a Hindu man could adopt a child from among his relations, who had the right to property, in the same way as would be given to his legitimate son. At times *gentios* transferred their movable wealth to *terra firme* to prevent it from being acquired by the Crown.

The plight of Hindu widows and daughters was distressing. Since they were not economically independent, they had to undergo great hardships. As per the custom of the land they could not remarry and some of these women, out of necessity got involved in prostitution. Therefore, the Church authorities prevailed on the Government, to come to the rescue of these women.

In 1542, Governor Martim Afonso de Souza, decreed, that in case a man died without a son, his movable property would go to widows and daughters, and the immovable one to the Crown. It appears that widows and daughters were not satisfied with what they received. They began making wider claims, leading the same Governor to issue one more decree in 1544, limiting the shares of the widows and daughters to 50 *pardaos,* in addition to houses (if they were covered with palm leaves), cattle, furniture and personal belongings. The immovable property would still go to the Crown (APO, V:175-177).

However, the above decree was not observed in practice. The conditions of the widows and orphans without fathers, continued to be distressing. Miguel Vas, Vicar General and Rui Barbosa, the *Pai dos Christaos* prevailed again on the Government, to come to the rescue of the widows and daughters by giving them property rights. This paved the way to a royal decree, issued by Dom Sebastiao in March 1559 (HAG:Ms.8791-RG-LV).

According to this legislation, widows and daughters of Hindus without male heir, were to get as much as was necessary for their maintenance, if they converted to Christianity. The sincerity of these people would be examined by the rector of the Jesuit College of St. Paul, Administrator of the Diocese and some others appointed for the purpose. Widows and daughters were to be given a period of six months to deliberate whether they wished to convert to Christianity. In case they decided not to embrace the new religion, the property of the Hindus without male heir would go to the next of kin, who was prepared to become a Christian. These relatives were to be given two months, to decide over the matter.

Few days later, another provision was issued. *Carta da Lei* dated 22nd March 1559, stated that the widow and the daughters of non-Christian men, who converted to Christianity, had the right to inherit the properties of their dead husbands and fathers, in case they died without male issue. This law was applicable to the inhabitants of city of Goa and other parts of Ilhas. Girls of Jewish origin were also entitled to similar rights. As in the case of previous ones, this too was not practiced. A Christian wife, in keeping with law, had equal interest in the property of her husband.

Non-Christians could not inherit from their Christian relations, whereas Christians could do so, from non-Christian family. In case, only child from a family, converted to Christianity, this child was immediately entitled to one-third of the family property and the child would inherit the remaining, on the death of his parent (Xavier 1861: 14-18).

The motives behind these reforms are questioned today. However, we must add here, that widows and orphans were given what was to be sold for the benefit of the Crown. These reforms benefited women, who converted to Christianity. It is quite possible, that many of Hindu widows and orphans ,might have taken advantage of these attractive laws which would help them to improve their conditions and make them financially sound.

The above mentioned laws, concerned widows and daughters who were orphans. What about women who converted to Christianity during the life time of their husbands ? The State tried, in 1562, also to safeguard their interests. Women who converted to Christianity, during the life time of their husbands, were entitled to jewellery and clothes they brought along at the time of marriage, and clothes they possessed at the time of conversion as well as half of both movable and immovable property (HAG:RG-LV:1/60v). This measure was necessary to encourage conversion, since many Hindu men retained the property when their wives converted to the new religion.

Despite the above mentioned laws safeguarding the interests of widows and orphans, it appears that widows and orphans continued to be deprived of their property rights. A royal *alvara* dated 1583 decreed, and reminded once again, that the property of Hindu man, should go to the widows and the daughters, in case they converted to Christianity, but if they refused, then it should go to the next of kin who converted to Christianity (HAG:PFC:51v-52). This was used as a bait to attract the natives to Christianity. The property of heirless (male) widows still would go to the Crown in case the family members refused to convert to Christianity. Therefore, the Hindus submitted a petition to the Viceroys D. Fernando Martins Mascarenhas and Luis Gonsalves Cotta, requesting that such property should not be acquired by the State.

Consequently, a Royal *alvara* of 1695, determined that Hindus of Goa (city of Goa), Salcete and Bardez should be governed by the Portuguese law, and the property of heirless (male) should not be acquired by the State. The same *alvara* gave widows the right to the property of their husbands and the daughters equal share with their brothers to their father's property. The Hindus were unhappy with the new *alvara*, that granted equal rights to the daughters They submitted yet another petition to the State informing that their earlier appeal was not properly understood — they did not ask for equal rights for their daughters but only rights in the absence of male child to prevent the property from being acquired by the Crown.

Hindus continued to follow their *Usos e Costumes*. As a result, Viceroy Conde de Sandomil requested the Crown to decide once and for all whether the *gentios* should follow their *Usos e Costumes* or the Portuguese law. In the meantime, a meeting of Hindus was convened to find out their opinion over the issue. The Hindus were divided in their opinion. Hindus with married daughters and sisters fearing that their husbands would claim property rights favoured *Usos e Costumes* as far as inheritance rights were concerned. Those who favoured the Portuguese law of inheritance were the husbands of married daughters and sisters.

The *regimento* of 1724 decreed that the daughters of non-Christians would have equal rights to their fathers' property only if converted to Christianity (APO,V:115). But few years later an *alvara* issued in 1739 decreed that the *gentios* of Old Conquests should be governed by Portuguese laws while their counterparts in New Conquests would be governed by their *Usos e Costumes*.

In order to protect the woman at the time of marriage and the property she owned at the time, the Portuguese Civil Code of 1867 gave women the choice of different ownership categories: Simple *Comunhao dos bens* (equal shares of assets from both the partners), second *separaçao dos bens*(separation of assets between the husband and wife) in this case she had to sign a contract, the third category was known as *regime dotal*. In the absence of any contract it was deemed that the marriage was done as per the custom of the country (CCP1956:388-389). The marriage as per the custom of the country consisted in the communion between the spouses of all their properties, present and future, not excluded by law. On the death of the husband, automatically, one half of his property would go to the wife. The rest of his property would be divided among his children of both the sexes. But at times, parents tried to avoid leaving married daughters their rightful share on the grounds that dowry was given to them at the time of marriage. Many times, this dowry was much less than their share of the family property.

The Civil Code, gave the husband all rights to administer the property that belonged to the couple. This right was introduced to preserve the economic stability of the family. The wife could do so, only in the absence of of the husband or in case of his inability. This clause recognized the husband as the head of the family and the stronger partner. However, the wife could reserve for herself, the right to receive a part of the income of her properties for pocket expenses, and dispose the same freely provided it did exceed one-third of the said net income.

The wife could be the administratix of the property, only during the absence or impediment of the husband, and could not alienate the immovable properties without the authorization of the family council, which would be assisted by the Public Prosecutor. The wife was not entitled to deprive the husband (by way of anti-nuptial contract) from administrating the properties of the couple.

The husband was not permitted without the consent of his wife, either to alienate immovable properties or to move the Court in respect of disputes regarding ownership or possession of immovable.

The authorization of the husband was required before the wife could acquire, alienate properties or contract obligations. In case the husband refused, the wife could still appeal to the respective Civil Judge to make it good and the judge could grant or reject it, as he thought fit, after hearing the husband.

The authorization of the husband was required for a wife to accept or renounce inheritance validly. The husband had to seek the consent of the wife in similar circumstances. The authorization of the husband and the consent of the wife had to be made good judicially.

A married woman could not be appointed as executrix without prior consent of the husband except when she was judicially separated from her husband and properties. Such authorization may be good judicially when the woman was married under the regime of separation of properties.

The consent of the husband was necessary for a married to make a will, unless she was married under the *separaçao dos bens* or officially separated from him. The wife could not incur debts without the prior permission of the husband except in his absence after proving the urgency or in case of the inability of the husband (CCP:305). A married woman was not permitted to buy or mortgage the property without the consent of the husband, except in exceptional circumstances permitted by law.

When a woman was accused of adultery, she was not entitled to separation of properties but only to maintenance, unless she could prove that at the time she committed adultery she could have applied for separation from her husband on any ground mentioned in clause no. 2 of article 1204.

The Civil Code safeguarded the interests of women in some instances. It enabled the wife married either under communion of properties or without it to apply for the separation of properties under custom of the country, under dotal regime, regime of the custom of country. She could take this step if she found herself in danger of losing whatever belonged to her, due to the bad administration by the husband. In case the separation materialized the wife was to be given the administration of the properties. The separation of properties did not exonerate the wife from contributing towards the expenses of the couple, from the income of her properties.

On the death of the husband the wife had the right to half of her husband's property and daughters and sons had equal shares. Girls at the time of marriage were asked to give *disistencia* (give up her share of property).

A widow who remarried would loose the right to *usufruto* and the right to administer properties of her minor children if so decided by the family council.

Polygamy Among Non-Christians

Polygamy was not uncommon among the Hindus, mainly of the upper strata, from the early period. The practice was accepted by the Hindu religion and the customs of the land. Hindu man, could have a second wife without divorcing the first one, specially if he had no male heir from the first wife (Xavier 1861). While Muslim men could have several wives according to their religion. A Muslim man could divorce his wife, by pronouncing *Talaq* three times in three different occasions in the presence of witnesses . This divorce was valid only as far as religion was concerned, by law Muslim men had no right to have a second wife.

The Viceregal decree of 1567 decreed monogamy for all irrespective of their religion (Boxer 1973:66-67). Men living with more than one wife or cohabiting with a concubine were ordered to dismiss all, except the one who they first married. Non-Christians often ignored the Viceregal decree and continued to marry more than one wife as permitted by their customs and traditions. Hindus of upper classes managed to get permission from the Government to perform *casamento simultaneo* (simultenous marriage) without divorcing the previous wife.

Since polygamy could not be completely abolished without hurting the feelings of the non-Christian inhabitants, the State tried to control polygamy in Portuguese India, through a *Carta Regia* dated 1614. Non-

Christians, desiring to have another wife, had to seek permission from the State (Xavier 1861). Those who violated this law were to be enslaved.

Ban on Child Marriage

The Portuguese Civil Code of 1867 decreed that women below the age of 12 years, could not marry. This law helped to reduce child marriages, specially in the colonies. Legally girls had to be married on reaching puberty. The Civil Code permitted for the first time in Portugal and her colonies the civil marriage, though it recognized the sacramentality of marriage in accordance with the Canon Law.

Under the Republic the age of marriage was further raised to 16 years for girls, and 18 years for boys, with the consent of the parents. Consent of the parents was required until the age of 21 years. Civil marriage, came now to be regarded as the only valid marriage for all purposes. Every individual had to perform the act of civil marriage before the religious marriage. It was the precondition for a religious ceremony.

In 1940 the Portuguese Government signed a *Concordata* with the Holy See. Recognition was given to religious marriage but religious marriage could not be solemnised by the Church without the no objection certificate from the competent authority at Civil Registration office. The religious marriage would have no civil effect without the transcription in the records of Civil Registration.

Rights and Duties of Women

The Portuguese Civil Code guaranteed equality to all, however, it recognized that in conjugal life, there existed inequalities between husband and wife.

According to the Civil Code of 1867 the wife had to obey the husband. This clause recognized the husband as superior partner. For instance, a married woman writer had to seek the consent of the husband before publishing her writings, but in case the husband refused to grant permission, she could still publish her work after getting the consent of the court. The wife had the duty of accompanying the husband wherever he lived, aside from a foreign country.

Prior consent of the husband was necessary for a married woman to move in the court. However, his consent was not required in criminal cases, in which she was the accused, in suit against the husband or in cases in which she had to exercise the rights and duties inherent in parental control, in respect of her legitimate issues, or of her illegitimate issues born from another.

The wife could enjoy all the honours of the husband, which are not merely inherent to the post he holds has held and could maintain them until she remarried.

The wife was forbidden from contracting and taking loans, without the prior permission of her husband. However, she was permitted to do so if the husband was away or was not in a position to do so. Women had no right to be witness at any will.

Under the Republic the married women gained several rights. It gave her more equality before men. The husband no longer could ask officially for the wife to be returned to him if she had no wish.

The Civil Code of 1867 had decreed that the wife had to obey the husband. This clause was erased under the Republic. It was now legally accepted that conjugal union was based on liberty and equality. However, the husband had to protect the wife, children and her property. The wife was in sole charge of the household affairs (*governo domestico*). It was her duty to strengthen the family unity.

The wife was permitted under the new Constitution to sue without the approval or permission of the husband, in the same way, that the husband could do, without the approval of the wife. The wife could now publish her writings without the prior consent of the husband. In order to maintain the family unity ,the new law ordered the wife to live with the husband, unless the husband, without her concurrence, desired to reside abroad.

Separation, Annulment, Divorce

The following were valid grounds for the separation of persons according to the Portuguese Civil Code: Adultery committed by the wife. Adultery of the husband with public scandal, or complete abandonment of the wife or keeping a mistress in the conjugal domicile. The conviction of the spouse to life imprisonment ill-treatment and serious injuries.

A man could seek a separation, if the wife committed adultery. However, the wife could ask for a separation only in case of adultery of the husband if it caused public scandal. There was no excuse for adulterous wife, even if her husband treated her badly. Adultery and unchastity in the woman, was a much more serious crime than in a man, before the society. The adultery in a man was not so sinful. This law did not equate the wife with the husband.

The Portuguese Civil Code of 1867 did not provide for a divorce. A Catholic marriage could be annulled only in the Ecclesiastical Court and in the circumstances contemplated in the laws of the Church followed in Portugal. The process was lengthy and complicated. The decision of the Ecclesiastical Court was to be executed by the Civil authorities.

Annulment of marriage gave both the partners right to remarry and had the same effect which are produced by dissolution of the marriage by death.

Divorce for the first time was permitted in Portugal after it became a Republic. Both the wife and the husband were entitled to seek divorce. The wife was entitled to claim maintenance from the husband, if in need of the same. A divorced woman could not remarry unless one full year had elapsed from the date of dissolution, while the husband could do so after six months of dissolution.

Widow Remarriage

Christian women in the seventeenth century, followed the Hindu practice of not remarrying after the death of the husband. Remarriages were frowned upon by the society and a few men were prepared to marry widows. Therefore, in 1684 Viceroy Francisco de Tavora, Conde de Alvor, issued an *Alvara de lei* declaring that those found preventing widow remarriages would be severely punished. Despite this *alvara* the practice of widows not remarrying continued in Goa.

According to the Portuguese Civil Code of 1867, a widow wishing to marry before the prescribed period of 300 days after the death of her husband had to undergo medical check up to rule out the possibility of being pregnant. Any person disobeying the order was liable to lose nuptial benefits, which, under the law or agreement, she had received or was to receive from her previous husband and these benefits would go to other legitimate heirs of the deceased.

Single Mothers

Single mothers and mothers of illegitimate children were protected under the Republic. Single mothers who were economically poor, had the right to ask maintenance from the father of the child and could claim compensation for all expenses incurred during the pregnancy and delivery. They could also ask for all the losses resulting from this fact Family Laws, (I: 151).

Widows, who remarried after fifty years of age, could not alienate, under any title, from the date of remarriage, the ownership of half the properties, when they had issues or descendants entitled to it.

Parental Control

Both parents were entitled to exercise control over minor children and protect them. Permission of the parents was required for marriage of children below 21 years of age. In case there was a disagreement among the parents, the opinion of the father prevailed.

Mothers were given right to participate in parental control by the changes introduced when Portugal became a Republic, but the right to exercise control, represent and defend minor children was given to the father who was the head of the family. The mother was given these powers only in the absence of the father.

The mother, who remarried, would lose the right to administer the property of minor children if not authorized to do so by the family council.

Hindu Women and Usos e Costumes

The Hindus from the early period were governed by *Usos e Costumes* of the land. These were guaranteed to them by the *Farol 1526* of Afonso Mexia. At the end of the seventeenth century, the Hindus of Old Conquests petitioned to the king that they should be brought under the general laws of the country. The request was granted to them in 1691.

In mid nineteenth century the Portuguese Government decided to compile and safeguard the *Usos e Costumes* of the *gentios* since it was connected with the Hindu religion and family organization. The *Codigo dos Usos e Costumes dos habitantes das Novas Conquistas* was promulgated in New Conquests in 1853. It safeguarded the usages and customs of the population of New Conquests but at the same time the code hampered the progress of Hindu women .*Codigo dos Usos e Costumes* differed from the general laws prevailing in the land specially concerning inheritance and rights of women. *Codigo dos Usos e Costumes* treated Hindu woman as an object without any rights.

In 1869 the Portuguese Government, after having introduced the Civil Code , felt the need to revise *Usos e Costumes* of non-Christina, so as to be, in conformity with the provision of the Civil Code. It was realized that it was not possible to abolish completely the *Usos e Costumes* of the non-Christian inhabitants of the land. The Hindu inhabitants had also requested the State to safeguard some of the provisions particularly concerning joint family, polygamy and adoption of a child. Therefore, the government decided to extend the Civil Code to the New Conquests as well, but at the same time, recognized their *Usos e Costumes* as far as marriages and some other matters were concerned. Accordingly, in 1880 the revised version was submitted for the Royal approval.

The new revised *Codigo dos Usos e Costumes* dealt mainly with marriage, divorce, adoption and property rights. As mentioned earlier in this chapter, Hindus were given a choice; if they wished they could opt out of the *Codigo dos Usos e Costumes* and seek justice under general Civil Code. The revised *Codigo dos Usos e Costumes* hardly improved the conditions of Hindu women.

Marriage and Remarriage under Usos e Costumes

A Hindu woman under *Usos e Costumes* could not marry after puberty while the man could marry at any age. The marriage of the Hindus, solemnized according to their religious rites, produced all civil effects which the laws of the nation acknowledged to Catholic and Civil marriages.

Codigo dos Usos e Costumes 1853 recognized polygamy among non-Christians. The *Codigo* was applicable only to the inhabitants of New Conquests, neverthelesss, the non-Christian inhabitants of Old Conquests also made use of this provision.

In 1880, when the *Codigo* was revised, the Government decided to control polygamy. Polygamy was recognized only in certain cases. A Hindu man could remarry without divorcing his previous wife in the following cases: (1) The first wife had no child when she reached the age of 25 years (2) Absence of male child after the first wife had completed thirty years of age and being of lower age, ten years had elapsed since the last pregnancy.(3) Separation of the marriage without male issue (4) Dissolution of the previous marriage. While Hindu man could remarry under these circumstances, the Hindu wife could not remarry during the life time of the husband. In fact, according to the customs of the land she was expected to remain faithful to him even after his death. In case a man desired to have a second wife the consent of the previous wife was required in the first two cases mentioned above. This consent had to be expressed in a public deed. Such consent was difficult to get, and often women were pressurized to grant the same. Today, a Hindu can still remarry under *Usos e Costumes* without divorcing the first wife, but they do not avail of such law. The general laws of the State are against polygamy.

The Hindu woman according to the *Usos e Costumes* had no right to seek divorce from the husband, but the husband could do so, in case the wife committed adultery, by justifying in the court and by performing a ceremony known as *gothacaria.* In such a case, the wife had the rights to maintenance benefits but in practice, a few wives were provided maintenance. Women were not educated, neither had they the courage to demand for their rights after being accused of adultery. She was usually thrown out of the house and considered non-existent, as far as the family of her husband was concerned. In addition, she would lose all that she brought from the house of her parents , or acquired during her marriage.

Widows, even if they had not reached puberty, could not remarry again. In case a Hindu man decided to take a widow as his wife, known as *mulher de pano,* such an union was not considered legal, nor the children born from such union were considered legitimate for any legal matters.

Hindu Women and Adoption

Hindu married women were not permitted to legitimate an illegitimate child but *bailadeiras* and other unmarried mothers as well as widows were permitted to do so. *Bailadeiras* were permitted to adopt a child from their own caste in case of the complete absence of issues.

Property Rights

According to the *Codigo dos Usos e Costumes,* things owned by the wife at the time of her marriage or what she acquired during her married life there, belonged to the husband.

A woman was not entitled to her family property but only for to maintenance and jewellery. Widow without children had the rights to the benefit of her husband's property during her life time. In practice she would hardly get anything from her joint family.

The wives of simultaneous marriages had jointly, the right to the moiety of inheritance of the common husband, subject to the ante- nuptial contract executed in terms of general law. Such moiety was to be divided in equal portions and in case of death of any one of them, her share was to devolve on her issues or respective heirs. The other half belonging to the husband would devolve, on his death, also in equal portions to the issues .

BAILADEIRAS DE GOA

The Portuguese were fascinated with the dancing girls. At times, they even neglected their duties and were responsible in delaying various expeditions in order to consort with these dancing girls. These women made use of their lovers, to often collect information for the enemies of the Portuguese. The situation caused much concern to the Portuguese authorities.

The Portuguese Government made attempts to curb the activities of the *bailadeiras,* throughout their rule, in this part of Portuguese Asia. The fact that several legislation to end the activities of the *bailadeiras,* were repeated throughout the period, and particularly in the seventeenth and eighteenth centuries, point out that the Portuguese were not successful in curbing the activities of these women. During the period under review, no measures were introduced to prevent exploitation of *bailadeiras* and to improve the conditions of these poor women.

One of the first decree promulgated by the Government to end such activities, was in the sixteenth century. It was a custom among the Hindus, to have *bailadeiras* performing dances at their weddings. This ban was lifted in 1555, during the time of Viceroy D. Francisco Barreto (ANTT: CGSO-IG: 36/5/3).

The ban was repeated by Viceroy Dom Constantino around 1560. Hindus were not only forbidden to have *bailadeiras,* but also to perform certain rituals at the time of the marriage. This order created a furor among the Hindus. The Hindus protested against the ban. Merchants from the island of Chorao (near City of Goa) and other places closed down their shops, some men sent their wives and children to the kingdom of Adil Shah, *rendeiros* threatened not to pay rents and the farmers opened up *valados* causing floods in the paddy fields. At the same time, Goa was surrounded by the enemy forces. Despite this situation, the Viceroy Dom Constantino refused to change his stand . He issued a strong *bando* (order) to the merchants, to open up their shops within specified time. The shops of those who refused, were to be confiscated and handed over to the newly converted Christians. The leaders of the revolt were ordered to leave the Portuguese territory, never to return again. Hindus who had migrated to Adil Shah's kingdom and failed to return within the specified time, were to be banned permanently from the Portuguese territory. Those who returned would be restored their confiscated property. The *bando* caused a terror among those who had revolted.

They immediately opened their shops, brought back their families, closed the *valados* and promised to pay rents (ANTT: CGSO-IG:36/5).

The *gentios* were unhappy with the situation. They were threatened and forced to obey the authorities. In 1578, these *gentios* sent a petition to the Crown, requesting to permit them to perform some of their customs, as it was being done in Salcete. This petition further complicated the situation. In 1579, the State not only refused permission to the inhabitants of city of Goa and adjacent islands but banned the practice in Salcete as well. Notwithstanding the ban, the Hindus continued to follow their customs at the weddings. This situation forced the Portugues sovereign to issue an *alvara* in 1681. The decree permitted them to perform their weddings, according to the customs of the land but behind the closed doors. The Hindus were further upset with the move. They decided to go to the enemy territory to perform their weddings according to their customs and traditions. These trips caused them much hardships and expenses. Often, the wedding parties were robbed on their way.

In 1598 nautch girls from the mainland were forbidden to come to the city of Goa and adjacent islands. Those disobeying the order, were fined 20 *pardaos* for the first time, 40 *pardaos* for the second time and the third time, such women were auctioned by the State.

These repeated bans had no effect on *bailadeiras* who continued with their traditional activities. Almost a century later the Viceroy of India issued another strong *alvara* banning *bailadeiras* from Goa. Nautch girls, including the ones from Maharatha and Moghul kingdom, found in Portuguese territories, would be killed (APO 1876: V).

In the eighteenth centuries several orders issued earlier were modified and new ones were enacted by the State to curb the activities of dancing girls in Portuguese India.

In 1700, the ban on *bailadeiras* was repeated. The inhabitants of Goa were once again banned from having *bailadeiras* in their homes, palmgroves or any other places. Heavy penalty was to be imposed on those who provided shelter to the dancing girls (ANTT: CGSO-IG, 36/5). The punishment varied according to the race and the community to which the guilty belonged. If he happened to be a *fidalgo* had to pay a fine of 100 *xerafins* for the work of Ribeira, in addition, he could lose many of his privileges and he could be exiled to any of the forts of the *Estado*. In case the guilty was a native Christian, he was to be beaten up and exiled to the galleys for a period of nine years. *Gentios,* found guilty of sheltering such women, would have their *xendy* cut off, beaten in public, and exiled to the galleys for a period of ten years (AHU:India-Caixa, 38/4). Apparently, the order was not strictly imposed, *bailadeiras* continued with their activities in Goa. In fact, they were patronized right from Viceroys to the soldiers.

The State banned again certain customs and practices at the time of Hindu marriages, particularly the custom of having *bailadeiras* to perform at the wedding. This greatly upset the *gentios*. They repeatedly sent petitions to the Portuguese Crown requesting permission to follow their customs and traditions. Consequently, *Alvaras regias* dated 1701 and 1704 permitted *gentios* to perform weddings with rituals, music, *and bailadeiras*, but with the condition that such weddings should be held behind the closed doors without the presence of Christians. The Hindus for sometime were not aware about the concession granted to them.

A royal letter of 1708 instructed the Viceroys to reinforce the ban on Christians attending dances performed by *bailadeiras,* under the penalty of being ex-communicated.(HAG: MR-72). This was followed by another letter the following year to Viceroy Dom Rodrigo da Costa to implement more strictly the royal order of 1704.

The patronage provided to these women by the Portuguese was not approved of by the higher clergy. Even though some of them were also accused of attending dances performed by the dancing girls. During this period, the Archbishops complained to the Crown about the activities of the officials with *bailadeiras.* On one occasion they were responsible for delaying the expedition to Muscat. On another occasion Viceroy D. Luis de Menezes, Conde de Ericeira (1717-1720) was accused of attending *aos bailes torpes das bailadeiras gentias na terra firme de Goa e tambem nas proprias terras do Estado.* His involvement with *bailadeiras* was one of the reasons, for losing his post. However, he was acquitted in 1736 and reappointed Viceroy of India.

Around 1726, soon after the Bicholim war, Viceroy Joao Saldanha da Gama, granted permission to some *bailadeiras* to enter the Portuguese territory but decided to restrict these women to certain areas. *Bailadeiras* were allotted the island of S. Estevam with the condition that they should live in houses covered with palm leaves. This measure was necessary to prevent the Portuguese from visiting these women in the enemy kingdom, since some of the Portuguese men were found carrying along gunpowder, cartridges and weapons for the enemy (APO, VI: 303). These were later used to fight against the Portuguese. *Bailadeiras* carried with them much wealth. The permission was revoked the following year by the Portuguese King D. Joao who was not happy with the new arrangements.

Bailadeiras continued dancing in public, at times even with the permission granted by the Viceroy himself. In 1729, one, Dessay Ramogy Rao of S. Mathias, was granted permission by the Viceroy to celebrate *sigmo* during Lenten season with music and *bailadeiras*(ANTT: CGSO-IG, 36/15). At the end of the same year Dom Joao forbade the celebration of *sigmo* during the Christian lenten season. The *alvara* also forbade celebrations at the wedding with music and *bailadeiras*.

As a result, viceregal decree dated 1730 ordered *bailadeiras* to leave the island of S. Estevam within 15 days. Those found returning to the island would be sentenced to death. The inhabitants were advised not to shelter them or hide them in their houses, palmgroves, shops, boats or induce them to come to the Portuguese territories even for few hours. The guilty, if he was a *Fidalgo,* could lose his jobs and could be exiled to Diu for a period of 5 years where he had to work without any salary. Natives were to be exiled for a period of 10 years. Furthermore, the *Ouvidor Geral do Crime* of Goa and the judges of Basçaim and Daman were ordered to carry out a survey every year in the month of February. The survey was to be conducted to ascertain the number of the people who sheltered such women or encouraged them in Portuguese India. They were empowered to take action against the guilty.

Despite the ban, *bailadeiras* continued living at S. Estevam as well as at Divar. In 1732 the Viceroy was complaining to the king about their presence in these islands with the permission granted by the king himself, on the advice of General Antonio Figueiredo Utra. Consequently, the ban on *bailadeiras* was repeated in 1734, during the time of Viceroy Pedro Mascarenhas, Conde de Sandomil. The *alvara* banned also young boys from dressing like *bailadeiras*. The guilty were exiled to Chaul for a period of five years with a fine of 500 *xerafins*. A third of the fine would go to the denouncer in case there was one and the remaining fine was to be used for the expenses of the Royal Treasury (APO VI).

In 1766 the inhabitants of Goa were appealing the Holy Inquisition, to permit them to have dancing girls and music for their weddings, according to the customs of the land. The Hindus often violated the ban. They continued to have their weddings in great pomp as can be concluded from a letter dated 1765 written by the Board of Holy Inquisition to the Viceroy Conde de Ega. However, in 1770 Ananta Camotim Vaga of Panelim was refused permission by the Holy Inquisition to celebrate a wedding in the family with musicians sent by the ruler of Sunda.

Finally, in 1930 the local Government decided to end the ceremony of *Xens* which initiated young girls into the life of *bailadeiras*. This legislation was the outcome of crusading efforts made by Rajaram Painginkar and others. As a result many of them left Goa and settled elsewhere in India, particularly in Bombay where they carried with their traditional activities.

SOLTEIRAS

Since the first century of the Portuguese rule in Goa, the Government appears to have been concerned about the prostitution in the city of Goa and other places. Several legislative measures were enacted to control the activities of the prostitutes and prevent sexually transmitted diseases.

By a royal letter dated 1593, King D. Filipe decreed that *solteiras* should live away from other people. They were forbidden to solicit on the streets and public places in the city of Goa. Prostitutes, found in other areas than the ones assigned to them, were to be fined 10 *pardaos*. Half to the accuser and the other half to the *meirinho* or captives. The executioner of justice, if found mixing with such women, would lose his job; he could be exiled to Ceylon for a period of five years and would have to pay a fine of 50 *pardaos*.

The decree had no desired effect on the life style of the prostitutes, who continued with their trade. They now began moving in palanquins from house to house. To end such a practice, King Filipe issued an order in 1597. By this legislation, individuals under 60 years of age were forbidden to move in palanquins, unless a special permission was sought from Viceroy Conde de Vidigueira. The guilty were to pay 100 *cruzados*. *Boyas,* found carrying persons below the age of 60, were to be sent to the galley. As in the case of the earlier legislation, the legislation of 1597 did not have the desired effect. In 1615, we have the Portuguese ruler, asking again the Viceroy D. Jeronimo de Azavedo to implement the order strictly. The order was repeated twice in the early seventeenth century.

Fifteen years later, in 1630, Viceroy Conde de Linhares was reminding the people not to use palamquins. Around this time the same Viceroy was writing to the king, informing him about the opposition he faced against the move, from Inquisitors, judges and other government officials. They complained about the ban on the use of palanquins, since they found it difficult to walk about in the city, on account of lack of transport. Further, Conde de Linhares was writing to the king, about the increase in venereal diseases, due to large scale prostitution. He was reminding him of the need to reinforce the law (Baiao 1949:I). The ban on the use of *palanquins,* was repeated in 1637 (ANTT: DRI: 40/169). The use of palanquins continued in vogue until the second half of the nineteenth century.

Since its efforts to curb prostitution did not work , the Government decided to legalize prostitution in the nineteenth century. The local Government issued two orders, one in 1879 and the other in 1898, legalizing prostitution in Portuguese India .

Prostitues were found near garrison areas in the capital city, and other places specially in Ilhas taluka. Portuguese soldiers were the ones who frequented these women while the officials preferred to keep mistresses.

Prostitution was responsible for the spread of syphilis and other sexually transmitted diseases in Goa. Venereal diseases continued to be common in the nineteenthth century among soldiers and others. Large number of soldiers were treated in the Hospital Militar for the same disease. In 1858 the Government repeated its order to Health Board making it compulsory to all prostitutes, to undergo weekly medical examination (Silva Gracias 1994). The following year, another order was issued to the Health Board to advise soldiers and others to stay away from the prostitutes (HAG: Ms.966 -COP: 122). It also asked to calculate funds necessary for the treatment of V. D. patients (HAG: Ms. 11668- CD:138).

Prostitution continued to be widespread in the tweentieth century in Portuguese India, around garrison areas and Marmugao port which was visited by foreign ships. The government made some feeble attempts to control the vice. The local Government changed its liberal attitude towards prostitutes. During the time of Governor Quintanilha Mendonça Dias it decided to revoke the orders issued in the nineteenth century, legalizing prostitution in Portuguese India. A legislative decree of March 1949, revoked the decrees of 1879 and 1898. The decrees were revoked because they were considered an insult to human dignity, to officially recognize prostitution.

In mid 1930's the State authorities with the help of Police tried to pressurize prostitutes to undergo medical check.

II. EDUCATION OF WOMEN

We have already noted earlier that in the first centuries of the Portuguese rule girls received no formal education. If they were given any education at all it was at home with the help of tutors. Female education in the early period was restricted only to the nuns of Santa Monica and the girls of *Recolhimento de Serra*.

Although girls received no formal education, irrespective of creed and caste, young Goan girls were imparted certain values. They were required to have certain accomplishments. At very early age they were educated to be good wives, housewives and mothers. In addition, Christian girls were provided religious education at the Church through out the Portuguese period just like their non-Christian counterparts were given religious instruction at home. In some upper class families, daughters were given lessons by a male teacher and learnt to play instruments like the tabla, piano,violin and other like instruments. They also learnt to sing *Mandes,* hymns and other songs. Girls were taught needle work, embroidery, crochet and lace-making. Girls from middle and lower middle class, spent their time profitably with needle work, lace making, making buttons and sewing clothes. Others distinguished themselves as medicine women and mid-wives.

In 1684, Viceroy Conde de Alvor had issued an *alvara* with the intention of promoting mixed marriages. The *Alvara* decreed, that all should speak Portuguese within a three years. This move, on the part of the Government, was supported by the Catholic Church in Goa because the Portuguese priests were reluctant to learn vernacular languages. The measure could not be implemented.

Until the mid nineteenth century, the State appears to have discouraged any move to promote women's education. Dom Francisco Manuel de Melo in his *Carta de Guia de Casados* had advocated that women's ability to read should be kept to the barest minimum. According to him the best book for women was the cushion and embroidery frame (Boxer 1975). Women were educated to be good housewives. Her role in life was to be a submissive wife and a good mother. Therefore, no measures were introduced to promote women's education, until the second half of the nineteenth century.

Instruçao Primaria (Primary Education)

In 1841, a *portaria* was issued, permitting the establishment in each town of a primary school for girls with a teacher and an assistant who would be paid 150 and 100 *xerafins* respectively. Notwithstanding the order nothing tangible emerged until 1846.

The first primary school for girls was established with great difficulties at Nova Goa (capital city) in 1846. Initially, there were no applicants for the post of a lady teacher. Very few women were educated at this time. These educated girls from upper strata did not work outside their home millieu.

Few years later, during the time of Viceroy de Vila Nova de Ourem, two more primary schools for girls were established, one at Margao (headquarters of Salcete taluka) and the other at Mapuça (Bardez). Teachers in each of these schools were paid a monthly salary of 20 *xerafins.* The education of women was completely neglected in New Conquests. Even in Margao and Mapuça, few girls availed themselves of the facilities offered. Parents were reluctant to send their daughters to school away from home. Apart from these primary schools, there were no other schools for girls in Goa.

In 1880's some primary schools provided education to boys as well as to the girls. Girl students at the primary level, in addition to reading and writing, learnt home science including dress-making and embroidery. A few girls sought admissions in these schools (Correia Afonso 1933). Singing and playing the piano was considered an asset for young Christian girls of upper and middle strata.

According to the Census of 1900 a total of 12,382 girls knew to read and write in Goa (Census 1900) Some of these were girls who knew to read and write in languages other than Portuguese. They knew to write and read in vernacular languages like Marathi and Konkani. A table in the appendix gives taluka wise literacy rate among Goan women in 1910 (See Appendix-1). The number of women who knew to read and write rose up to 16,337 in 1910 and to 17,357 in 1921(Census 1921). By 1940 the number of girls who could read and write, was estimated to be 21,963 (Census 1940). The Census of 1950 reveals that a total of 53,591 girls knew to read and write, out of these some 18,314 knew to write and read in Portuguese (Census 1950). The Old Conquests had the highest number of literate women. Among the Old Conquest talukas, Bardez had a high literacy rate. Probably, due to male immigration to Bombay, East Africa and Burma. This brought the people in greater contact with outside world and gave the inhabitants better economic conditions. Consequently, many parents started sending their young daughters to school. The ability to read and write helped women to communicate with their husbands, fathers and brothers who were absent from their homes for a considerable time. In 1940 about 8,789 girls from Bardez taluka knew to read and write.

In the early decades of the twentieth century, several schools were opened in different parts of Goa. For instance, in 1909, two schools were opened — one at Cansaulim in Salcete taluka and the other at Calangute (Bardez). Therefore, the existing school for girls at Calangute, subsidized by the Bardez Municipal Council, was moved to Anjuna village in the same taluka.

In the second decade of the twentieth century, daily newspapers and periodicals such as *O Indispensavel,* carried out a campaign to educate women. Families that were undergoing a process of modernization, began to send their daughters to schools. Some of these schools provided education in Portuguese while others in Marathi and English. Periodicals of the 1930's like *Mascote* made the society and mainly the parents, aware of the need to educate women. The aim was to make women economically independent. In the last few decades of the Portuguese rule in Goa many girls went in for higher studies in medicine and teaching.

A decree issued in 1956, made primary education compulsory to both boys and girls between the ages of seven and thirteen (LREI 1956). A fine of 500 escudos was to be imposed on those who did not follow the order.

In addition to schools imparting primary education in Portuguese, there were schools providing education through Marathi and English medium. Hindu girls attended Marathi schools. English schools provided education upto High School level and prepared students for Secondary High School Examination. Many of the English schools were affiliated to various Secondary School Boards in India. These schools were popular with Goans who had families outside Goa.

Colegio de Nossa Senhora de Piedade

This was the first *colegio* started in 1887, to provide education for girls. The institution was started due to initiative of *Santa Casa de Misericordia da Goa.*

Earlier attempts made by Jose Inacio de Loiola and others to establish *colegio* for girls elsewhere in Goa, received no cooperation from the State. In fact, colonial politics killed a plan made by Viscount de Sao Januario in 1871. According to this plan each taluka of the Old Conquest would have a *Colegio* for girls.

Colegio de Nossa Senhora de Piedade was run by *Irmas Hospitaleiras.* The institution had students from upper and middle strata of the society. The Recolhimento de N. Sra. de Serra also sent its inmates to this institution for learning. They were sent in batches of twelve. Besides primary education in Portugues, there was a language course in French and English. Students were taught about history, geography, grammmar and arithmetics (LREI 1905). In addition, girls were taught to sing and play the piano. Separate courses in embroidery, dress making , flower making, cookery and painting were also conducted for girls in this institution. Students were admitted in this school between the age of 5 to 18 years. The applicants at the time of admission had to provide a certificate from a government doctor stating that they did not suffer from any contagious diseases. The school provided hostel facilites for the students and preference was given to destitutes ana orphans.

The institute was in charge of a *Regente* and under the supervision of a committee comprising of *Reitor of Liceu Nacional*, Inspector of Primary Education, and Director of *Escola Normal*

The constitutional change in Portugal in 1910 had its impact on women's education in Goa. The Republican Government, who was against congregations, issued orders to close down *Colegio de N. Sra. de Piedade*. However, the institution was replaced by *Escola Nacional do Sexo Feminino* in 1911. The following table porvides the number of students admitted at the school between 1911 to 1921 for different courses.

Year	No. of girls
1911	10
1911-1912	81
1912-1913	54
1913-1914	94
1914-1915	155
1915-1916	150
1916-1917	156
1917-1918	129
1918-1919	165
1919-1920	161
1920-1921	241

A legislative decree, issued in 1931, restricted the number of the students admitted for each of the course. Twelve girls could be admitted at a time in dress making course. For piano course the number was fixed for five girls, while in the language course, 20 girls could be admitted at a time (LREI 1931).

In 1952, the school was renamed again as *Instituto de N. Sra. de Piedade*. The institution was handed over to the Archbishop who asked the sisters of Sacred Heart of Mary to run the institution. The course imparted at this Institute was reorganized by the Central Government in 1953. According to the decree of 1953, the students had a choice cf three courses: (1) Housewife course of one year, (2) Family education course of two years, (3) Family and Social Worker Course of three years. The *Housewife course* consisted of the following subjects: Home science, religion, horticulture,tailoring, cooking, physical education, family and social education, hygiene and nursing. Besides these subjects, in the second course, students were also given some ideas about civics and social behaviour. The third course was a combination of the first two. In 1955 the *Colegio de N. Sra. de Piedade* had a total of 137 students, out of these 45 were living in the institution.

Instituto Dona Amelia

In 1894 *Instituto Dona Amelia d'Orleans* was started for girls in Margao by Manuel Agostinho Lourenco (nephew of Dr. Agostinho Vicente Lourenço). The institute closed down when its founder migrated to Brazil.

Higher Secondary School

In the nineteenth century there was one Higher Secondary School, *Liceu Nacional,* in the capital city. *Liceu Nacional* was open to students of both sexes, yet hardly any girl availed themselves of this opportunity in the nineteenth century. In a few cases girls were prepared at home and appeared for the public examination of *Liceu*. Parents were reluctant to send their daughters to school due to the attitude of the society which believed that a girl's place was at the home and she did not require formal education. In addition, lack of transport facilities and economic conditions might have contributed to lack of female students.

In the first academic year of the twentieth century , *Liceu Nacional* Panjim had one girl student. The number went gradually increasing. In the academic year 1907-1908 there were two girls in the school. A total of 9 girls studied in the school during the academic year 1911-1912. This number went up to 19 girls in 1916.

In 1913 *Liceu Municipals* in similar lines were estblished in Margao and Mapuça. Some girls joined these institutions. The number of girls was higher in Margao. *Liceu Municipal* of Margao had a total of about 333 girls between 1914-21, while the one in Mapuça had around 93 students during the same period.

In the early decades of the twentieth century, girls especially from Salcete, attended *Curso Preparatorio* at Rachol Seminary. Some others appeared for examination in French and Latin subjects conducted by the same Seminary.

Newspapers and periodicals carried out a campaign in the early decades of the twentieth century, about the need to promote women's education in Goa, specially in sciences, so that they could be brought on par with the men and to make them economically independent. The lack of adequate education for girls was discussed at various *Congressos Provinciais* held in Goa, in the first three decades of the twentieth century. Many of the participants of second *Congresso Provincial,* expressed the need to promote women's education beyond the elementary level. At the same Congress, a suggestion was made for the establishment of a *colegio* for girls at the capital city of Panjim, Margao (south Goa) and Mapuça (north Goa). The aim was to prepare the girls to be good housewives by providing elementary education and knowledge of home science. The establishment of schools for girls in all villages of the Old Conquests was discussed at the Congress.

The nineth *Congresso Provincial* discussed also the problems faced by Hindu girls in the field of education. Hindu girls of upper strata of the society were sent to Marathi school upto the age of 11 years. While Hindu boys after completing their primary education in Marathi joined Portuguese schools, Hindu girls stayed at home after the age of 11 years. They were not provided further education as most of them were married by the time they were fourteen years old. Suggestions were made by one of the participants, to start a school where these young girls could be taught home sicence and literature in addition to the elementary education. It was expressed that a more complete education would help the girls to be good wives, mothers and good members of the society.

Women's education left much to be desired in the third decade of the twentieth century. Education of women of upper middle strata was not paid much attention to and that of the lower strata, was completely neglected. It was felt that many women of lower strata given the opportunity, could do as well as the women of upper classes. It was suggested that Sunday classes should be held for economically deprived women. These Sunday classes were to be held in Konkani in each village and were to be supported by *Junta Locais*. Further, it was suggested that in addition to reading, writing and arithmatic, the girls should be given some knowledge of hygiene, needle work, cottage industries, horticulture and animal husbandry. Similar classes were held at this time in British India with great success.

Lack of adequate educational institutions in Goa forced some progressive parents to send their young daughters to far away Bangalore, Belgaum, Bombay and Pune for further studies. This imposed an additional economic burden on the parents. They spent on average Rs. 30-35 a month on their wards, studying outside the territory. The sum spent for two years would be sufficient to impart similar education in Goa for three years, if it was available.

Propercia Correia Afonso de Figueiredo, who was concerned about the education of women in Goa, proposed the idea of starting a *Liga Femenina*. She proposed that each member of the *Liga* should select a girl and teach her to read and write in her mother tongue Konkani. The girl was also to be taught dress-making. The selected student had to be above ten years of age and had to be a daughter of an uneducated mother. Another suggestion made was to teach a non-Christian girl Konkani in Roman Script and learn from her the Devanagiri Script.

Nursing Courses

In the present century, girls joined the nursing courses attached to *Escola Medico-Cirurgica de Goa*. Initially girls from upper strata did not join the course. Work outside the home was commonly regarded as unsuitable to women other than those of the lower classes. Fortunately, this attitude changed in course of time. In 1916 when the local Government approved a new syllabus for the Nursing Course, it made provisions for crash courses in Portuguese for Hindu girls, who had no knowledge of the language (LREI 1916). Hindu girls without primary education, but possessing other requirements were allowed to join the course in midwifery. They were to be trained in Konkani and Marathi (LREI 1917).

Hospital de Misericordia of Ribandar had a nursing course for the orphan girls from *Recolhimento de N.Sra de Serra*, an institution attached to *Santa Casa de Misericordia*. From 1922 this course was open to all girls irrespective of caste, creed and colour (BO 1922: no. 62).

In 1920 Dr. Inacio Manuel Miranda was granted permission by the Government to start a nursing course at Hospicio de Sagrado Coraçao, Margao. This was necesssary due to high maternal mortality rate, acute shortage of nurses and midwives to provide care for the inhabitants of Goa (LREI 1920).

According to a decree issued in 1958, girls with S.S.C. (School Secondary Certificate) or technical course could also be admitted for the nursing course. Similar concession had been granted two years earlier to girls desirous of joining the course of midwives (LREI 1958).

Vocational Course

In the last decades of the Portuguese rule in Goa some technical schools were setup in major towns of Goa. Young girls and boys were imparted vocational education.

Higher Studies

Two institutions of higher studies were started in the nineteenth century in the capital city of Goa. These schools were *Escola Medico-Cirurgica de Goa* and *Escola Normal.* These two schools were opened for students of both sexes, yet initially girls did not join the institutions.

The first school (*Escola Medico-Cirurgica de Goa*) of western medicine in Asia was opened in 1842 at the Military Hospital in Nova Goa (Silva Gracias 1994). Earlier the informal education of medicine was carried out at the Royal Hospital in the city of Goa. In the beginning of the twentieth century *Escola Medico-Cirurgica de Goa* did not have single woman student. The first woman to graduate from *Escola Medico-Cirurgica de Goa* was in 1910.

The second institution of education was *Escola Normal*–training school for primary teachers. The school was established in mid nineteenth century. When it was reorganized in1907 a lady teacher was appointed among its staff. This appointment helped to attract admission from girl students.

In the last decades of the Portuguese rule in Goa, a number of girls continued with higher studies in medicine, pharmacy and teaching in Goa .Unfortunately, the choice of courses was very limited and some had to migrate elsewhere in India for further studies.

The Portuguese throughout their rule passed a number of legislations to uplift the conditions of Goan women, particularly in the nineteenth and twentieth centuries. The first to benefit were Christian women. The Hindu women legged behind because they were governed by their *Usos e Costumes*. However, they were given an option at the end of the nineteenth century, they could opt out of their Hindu Law and seek application of the general Portuguese law. Attention to the education of Goan women was paid only at the fag end of the Portuguese period.

5

GOAN WOMEN AS REFLECTED IN CHURCH DECREES AND INSTRUCTIONS

During the Portuguese rule in Goa, the Christian Church played a significant role not only in spreading the Christian religion in this part of Asia, but also in spreading a culture that was evolved in the West. The new culture brought about social changes in Goa and led to the mingling of the East and West.

The Christian Church in Goa gained importance after 1577, when it was raised to the rank of the metropolitan Archdiocese. The Archdiocese of Goa embraced the whole of East from the Cape of Good Hope (Africa) till China. In the early centuries of the Portugüese rule, the Christian Church in Goa was a powerful institution–it was a State within the State. The Church provided funds to the State. In the early period the Church was headed by a Vicar General, than by Apostolic Commisssarie, Bishops, Archbishops and finally after 1886 by Patriarchs. Archbishop and the Patriarchs were appointed by the Portuguese Crown on approval from the Pope.

The Church brought about socio-religious changes through decrees issued by Church Provincial Councils, Pastoral letters and the Holy Inquisition. Church Provincial Councils were held in 1567, 1575, 1583, 1592, 1606 and another one held almost three centuries later in 1894.

Decrees were issued to regulate the activities of the faithful, to regulate their morale as well as to prevent them from following certain non-Christian customs. Customs which were seen as problems for the practice of new faith. Non-Christians were also at times subject to these decrees which were executed by secular authorities.

Some modern historians have accused the Church in Goa of exploiting the women socially and economically. Was this really true? The Catholic Church in Goa introduced several reforms to uplift the conditions of women and to give them better quality of life (See Appendix 2). The Church influenced also the State to introduce reforms to improve the position of women in Goa.

At times the Church had ulterior motives, as for instance when the Church imposed certain restrictions on women with the intention of preventing them from being influenced by non-Christian customs and traditions. Customs which could affect and change their attitude towards the Church. Bans were imposed against some non-Christian customs followed at the time of births, marriages and deaths (Appendix 3). The Holy Inquisition punished and imposed heavy penalties on women following some non-Christian traditions (Appendix 4). Sometimes in order to introduce these changes, penalties were imposed. Nevertheless, after all that has been said the Christian Church showed concern about the plight of the Goan women.

This chapter has two parts. Part I consists of reforms introduced by the Church to improve the conditions of women during the colonial period. Part II deals with the institutions established by the Christian Church to help women and the role of the Church in women's education.

I. CHURCH DECREES ON WOMEN DURING THE COLONIAL RULE

Polygamy and Early Marriages

The Church was concerned with polygamy among the Hindus in Goa. This encouraged infidelity and it was considered a bad example to the newly converted Christians. Besides, this was an impediment to the conversion of non-Christians, since the Church was against polygamy and on conversion the person would be asked to have only one wife. The First Provincial Council (1567) requested the State to forbid Hindu man from having more than one wife or mistress. The State acting on the advice of the First Provincial Council (1567) decided to abolish polygamy. This received the sanction of law by Viceregal decree of the same year. Those violating the law were to be enslaved. In practice the ban was ignored. Therefore, in 1606 the Fifth Church Council renewed its appeal to the Government to impose punitive measures against those who committed polygamy or kept mistresses. The Church Council requested the Portuguese authorities to punish non-Christians who had many wives or mistresses.

Early marriages were also the cause of concern to the Church. In 1787, an episcopal decree disapproved the custom followed by native Christian parents of marrying their daughters when they completed 12 years of age. The Church was of the opinion that girls at this age were very young to undertake their married responsibilities. Parents were advised to marry their daughters at slightly higher age when they were mature to understand the meaning and responsibilities of marriage (SCD 1900:28).

Ban on Practices During Pregnancy and Child Birth

As stated earlier in this work, a wide spread custom required that the pregnant woman returned to the house of her mother for the birth of the first child. A *primagravida* was taken to the home of her parents well in advance, normally two to three months before delivery and they stayed with the parents at least one month after delivery. As a result, married women stayed away from their husbands for a long period of time. Therefore, an Episcopal decree dated 1604 advised women to co-habit with their husbands during their pregnancy. This measure was implemented to keep the young couple together and to prevent problems caused by their separation.

During the major part of the colonial rule, deliveries were performed at home and attended by a *dai.* The First Church Council held in 1567, prevented Christian women from seeking help of Hindu *dai* at the time of child birth because they used non-Christian rituals and witchcraft (BP 1889:138). In 1785 Margarida Borges, a *dai* by profession from S. Bartholomeo (Chorao) was punished by Holy Inquisition for practicing superstitious rituals at the time of delivery. As a punishment she was sent to *Casa da Polvora* for 5 years(ANTT:CGSO-IG: 33/19). Another dai Catharina (Boteli) was also accused by the Holy Inquisition of practicing superstitious rites at the time of delivery.

The Fifth Church Council banned women to have *vigias* at the time of delivery, and to follow non-Christian practices. The guilty were to be punished with ex-communion and a fine of 40 *pardaos* in case of Portuguese whites, the natives were to be fined 20 *pardaos.* Half of the amount would go to the denouncer.

It was a custom to engage a wet nurse to nurse the child, probably because mother's milk was not sufficient. Repeated pregnancy might contributed to the problem. The Fifth Church Council forbade women under penalty from engaging wet nurses for their infants. A Christian woman engaging a Hindu wet nurse was to be fined 50 *pardaos,* if the wet nurse was a Muslim in addition to the fine, the person engaging the wet-nurse could be ex-communicated.

A decree issued in 1736 by the Holy Inquisition banned the practice of celebrating the sixth day of the birth (ANTT:CGSO-IG:36/23). The same decree forbade a postpartum practice of having bath near the well for a period of two months. Many times betel and areca nut was mixed in the water. This was a non-Christian practice followed by Christian women.

Christian women like their Jewish counterparts did not attend Church services for 40 days after the delivery. They were instructed by the decree not to follow the same, but despite the instructions they continued with the practice. In 1784 an Episcopal decree again instructed the Parish priests to advise women to go to the Church before 40 days. These bans were disregarded by Christian women.

The Response of the Church to Sati

Sati was abolished by Albuquerque and the ban repeated by Dom Constatino in 1560, but despite the ban the practice continued for a long time in some parts of Goa. The Third Church Council prevailed on the Government to end the practice and to encourage widow remarriage. Those who were forced to follow the evil practice, were to be punished and the fine collected from them were to be used for *Obras Pias* (Works of Charity). The Church has been accused of ulterior motives in this matter.

Concern for the Widow

By and large the Church appears to be concerned with the deplorable conditions of the widows both Christians and non-Christians.

The Church appealed several times to the Government to improve the conditions of widows. The Church Provincial Councils repeatedly asked the local authorities to ban the practice of tonsuring the widows and to promote widow remarriage. The Second Church Provincial Council held in 1575 tried to prevail on the Government to ban Hindu women from shaving their hair, after the death of their husbands (BP 1889). It also asked the same authority to impose heavy fine on those who prevented widow remarriages. Customs and traditions banned Hindu women from remarrying. The property of the accused who prevented remarriages was to be confiscated. Half of this property would go to the denouncer and the other half to *Obras Pias*. However, the State did nothing about the problem and the Third Church Council (1583) decided to renew the appeal. It is possible that the State was reluctant to introduce measures that would hurt the feelings of non-Christians.

Eventually, the Episcopal decree of 1604, ordered that widows below the age of forty should be encouraged to remarry one year after the death of their husbands. Those who did not wish to marry were to be sent to city of Goa to live with some honest Portuguese or native families. Probably, to work as servants in the houses of these families. The number of widows during this period was large. Girls married early and many of them lost their husbands when still young. Since they could not remarry according to prevailing customs and traditions, they were condemned to a life of misery as they were not economically independent.

Finally, the Fifth Provincial Council issued a decree that no woman should shave her hair after the death of the husband, as a sign that she could not remarry. Only women above 50 years were allowed to do so. The above applied to Christian women as well. Apparently, the Christian widows also followed this practice.

In spite of these decrees the conditions of the widows did not improve in practice. Tonsuring continued in Goa among the Hindus for a long time and widow remarriages were frowned by the society.

Poor socio-economic conditions of widows forced some of them into prostitution and casual sex. The Church showed its concern. Documentation available for the eighteenth and nineteenth centuries shows that the Church tried to control such activities. During the Pastoral Visits of Archbishops to different parishes under its jurisdiction several widows were accused of being involved in casual sex. They were reprimanded by the Archbishop through the Parish Priests.

One widow at Betalbatim was accused of killing her illegitimate child soon after birth. When she conceived again she left the village to avoid being reprehended by the Parish priest. She returned after some months showing no signs of the pregnancy. In 1771, a Kunbi widow was accused of getting pregnant for the second time and for throwing her foetus for the pigs to eat (PP:VP13-15/49-51). Yet another widow by name of Maria from Britona was beaten and ordered to attend the Church with her head uncovered for having given birth to a child. This punishment was imposed during the pastoral visit of 1779 (PP:VP16-17/10v-11).

Property Rights

According to the customs of the land, non-Christian widows and daughters had no right to the property of their husbands and fathers. In 1542, Miguel Vas, the Vicar General secured a provision from Governor Martim Afonso de Souza. By this provision the movable property of the deceased without the male heir would go the widows and daughters if they converted to Christianity. However, the Hindus found means and ways to avoid implementation of such orders. This caused great hardships to widows and orphan girls. Consequently, Miguel Vas in a letter to the Portuguese ruler, suggested that daughters should be given entire property. He was hoping thereby to get more converts to his religion.

It appears that the State did not take any action in this direction. In 1548, we have again Rui Barbosa (Pai dos Cristaos) complaining to the Portuguese sovereign Dom Joao III, that many souls are lost because daughters were denied their share of property. In the same letter he tried to explain how the king was not getting anything from these properties. The property was auctioned to the village elders according to the custom of the land. The proceeds were used to pay off the debts of the deceased and the remaining would go to the Crown. Property which was worth something was given away by the State to those having large holdings, whereas the ones that measured little were distributed among native officials (Costa 1965). In practice no property remained with the Crown. Therefore, the Crown had nothing to loose by giving women right to the property of their husbands and fathers.

In 1567, the First Church Council also requested the Crown to enforce more strictly the existing law permitting widows to inherit their husbands' property if converted to Christianity.

Escravas

In the early period the Church did not condemn slave trade carried out by Christians. In fact, Jesuit missionaries in Goa kept slaves and were involved in large scale slave trade with Japan and Africa during the early centuries of the Portuguese rule in *Estado da India* (HAG: Ms. 2088-Receita e despeza de Jesuitas). The Church did not see great evil in slavery. Nevertheless, it tried to check slave trade carried by non-Christians.

The First Church Council forbade the export of slaves by non-Christians. Captains of ships helping traders were to be ex-communicated by the Church and fined 50 *pardaos.* The same Council passed a resolution demanding freedom to those slaves owned by non-Christians who converted to Christianity. None of these resolutions were implemented.

It must be said to the credit of the Church that it did take interest in well being of the slaves employed in domestic service in Portuguese India. The Church was concerned about the conditions of the slaves and the treatment meted out to them by their masters. Several European travellers' accounts and other documents of the sixteenth and seventeenth centuries provide to us detailed information about the conditions of the slaves in Goa. Mortality rate among the slaves was very high. When a slave fell sick, the slave was thrown out by the master to die on the streets. The practice was banned by the Church Councils. The Council requested *Santa Casa de Misericordia* to provide shelter to the poor slaves.

The First Church Council banned without much success corporal punishment to slaves. The Third Church Council forbade the following forms of punishment against the slaves: beating with cane stick, applying hot iron rods, keeping slaves hanging upside down, pouring vinegar, chilies and salt in the eyes of the slaves besides *todas as formas refinadas de tortura,* (Boxer 1990) but neither this ban nor subsequent ones helped to improve the conditions of the slaves as can be seen from available historical literature of the period.

The free life style of the slave women led the Church to impose restrictions on their movements. It was decreed by Fifth Church Provincial Council that slave women below 50 years of age should not be engaged in selling goods on the road side, neither they should spend the night out of their homes. But like some previous orders concerning slaves this one too was ignored by the slave masters who depended for their living on the earnings of their slaves. The same Council banned captains of ships and the crew from carrying female slaves on board.

During the early period of colonial rule it was not uncommon for men to have slave girls in their homes working as cooks. The Fifth Church Council forbade married men (who lived without their wives), widowers and bachelors from employing female slaves below fifty years as cooks.

In 1725 Archbishop D. Inacio de Santa Tereza was complaining about the treatment meted by *senhoras* to their female slaves. Many of these ladies encouraged their husbands to cohabit with the slave girls, while others were so jealous of these relationships that they used to beat slave women to death and bury them in the courtyards at night.

The breasts of some of these slaves were cut off, the flesh minced and used to make patties. These patties were given to unsuspecting husbands to eat. Some mothers encouraged their sons to have affairs with slave girls at home rather then visit prostitutes, probably on account of large incidence of venereal diseases in the city and other reasons.

Solteiras

As we have seen earlier in this work, prostitution was responsible for moral degradation and diseases specially among the Portuguese in Goa. Prostitution was common in the city of Goa and other places.

The Church Council in 1567 advised the Municipal Council to set aside fixed areas for prostitutes beyond the Hospital of St. Lazarus in the city of Goa. Those disobeying the order were to be exiled for five years to Ceylon and fined 50 *pardaos.* The legislation was not strictly implemented.The demand was repeated by the Fifth Church Council in 1606, with instruction that the order should be implemented by the Parish priests.

Non-Christian women of ill fame were prohibited from living with Christian women. The Fifth Church Council ordered that the former should live separately beyond the Hospital of S. Lazarus in the city of Goa. Due to widespread prostitution the Fifth Church Council forbade women from moving about in palanquin. A fine was imposed on those found doing so.

The Church Councils were not the only ones to issue decrees to control the activities of prostitutes. Very often the Archbishop issued decrees. There were also measures passed at the time of Pastoral visits to Parishes in Goa. These measures were applied to specific villages. The sentences were executed by the Parish priest or his assistant. Non-Christians who lived in predominantly Christian areas were also subjected to checks imposed by the Archbishop but these checks were executed by secular authorities.

During the Pastoral visit of 1748 several women of Mormugoa were accused of offering their services to Frenchmen (sailors) and Portuguese soldiers (PP: VP I,V,VI). Portuguese officials were also accused of having *bailadeiras* in their residences. In 1771 Rosa from Orlim (Salcete) was accused of living for two years with Severino, a Portuguese soldier stationed at Cabo da Rama. Rosa gave birth to male child from this relationship. She was advised to confess and marry the man, on the contrary both would be severely punished. In some cases the accused were asked to pay fine.

Parents and siblings of young girls were often accused of encouraging their daughters and sisters into prostitution. During the Pastoral Visit to Margao in 1772, a woman Ignacia whose husband was away was accused of offering her adopted daughter Mariana for prostitution (PP:VP:13-15/22).

Visitas Pastorais refer also to instances when husbands encouraged their wives to go into prostitution, probably ,due to economic problems. There are cases when prostitutes worked as cooks and maids in the houses of their masters. Penalties were imposed on those indulging in prostitution. They were fined, imprisoned, beaten up, their hair shaved off and sometimes sent away from their villages. Usually the ones from Bardez(north Goa) were sent to Salcete (south Goa) and *vice-versa.* At times some these women were sent to Portuguese possessions in Asia and Africa.

Casual Sex

Casual sex prevailed among the lower class people. A woman from Ecoxim was accused of adultery with a surgeon from Chorao (Ilhas) during the Pastoral visit to the Parish of Pomburpa (Bardez). As a punishment he was exiled to Tiracol (Pernem) and she was sent for a period of ten years to Benaulim (Salcete). In addition, both had to pay fines.

Emigration of Goan men to British India, Africa and other places for a considerable length of time, sometimes endangered the bonds of fidelity in marriage. Some women whose husbands were way, were accused of adultery in the absence of their husbands, as in the case of one Maria wife of Manoel Roiz who was working in Ghat area (PP:VP: 7-8). These women were ordered as punishment to attend Church services on the days of obligation with their heads covered.

A decree issued by the Church in 1868 forbade priests to have women in their houses as cooks and paying guests. Close relatives of the opposite sex were also forbidden from staying in the Parish house for long period of time.

Prostitution and casual sex were responsible many times for abortion. Several factors forced women to resort to abortion. Among others was the attitude of the society towards unwed mothers and illegitimate children. A stigma was attached to them. Besides, women were not economically independent neither they had the courage to defy the society. Consequently, some women resorted to abortion which was disapproved by the Church and society. Therefore, those who wished to abort resorted to quacks. Various methods were used to get rid of the foetus. These quacks who were responsible for permanent damages and even death.

Bailadeiras de Goa

Bailadeiras were the favourite theme of the Indo-Portuguese poets and writers. They were also the subject of much correspondence between the State and the Church. The Christian Church in Goa appears to have been concerned with the effect *baladeiras* had on men and in particular on Portuguese men in Goa. Several attempts were made by the Church to curb the activities of *bailadeiras.* As an upholder of moral order the Church believed it was her duty to bring to the notice of the government the activities of these *bailadeiras* and mainly their activities with the Portuguese men.

The Fifth Church Council determined that *bailadeiras* should not participate in processions. Punitive measures were to be taken against those encouraging such participation. The same Council banned dancing schools that trained *bailadeiras* in dancing.

In the end of the seventeenth century Archbishop D. Frei Agostinho de Anunciaçao, issued a *Pastoral* banning *bailadeiras* from performing in public. During the same period the Archbishop was writing to the king to reinforce the ban against their activities or to force them to attend instructions in the Church every Sunday and holydays. The Portuguese King Dom Joao V did not favour such measures. He was of the opinion that religion could not be imposed by force on people. Nevertheless, he was seized with the problem – he was concerned about the influence of *bailadeiras* on Portuguese men in Portuguese India. In 1699 he induced the Viceroy to issue an *alvara* forbidding *bailadeiras* to live within the Portuguese territory.

Throughout the eighteenth century, we have the Church authorities complaining to the secular authorities in Goa and Lisbon about the activities of the dancing girls with Portuguese men. Eventhough, at times Church authorities, *Inquisidores* and others in Goa were also accused of attending dances performed by *bailadeiras* (ANTT:CGSO-IG:31/2).

In early eighteenth century, the Archbishop was writing to the home authorities about the encouragement given to *bailadeiras* by the local authorities including the Viceroy Melo e Castro. Consequently, on the advise of the Church , a Royal letter dated 1708 reminded the Viceroy to reinforce more strictly the ban on *bailadeiras.* Despite this order and subsequent ones, local authorities continued to patronize these women for several years more in Valverde (Bardez) and other places. *Fidalgos* in the Provincias de Norte also kept bailadeiras as mistresses. This paved the way for the enactment of two well known alvaras in 1700, banning bailadeiras from Goa.

In 1725 , the Archbishop was reminding again to the Crown about the patronage provided by the Portuguese officials to dancing girls. Many of these officials neglected their duties to be with bailadeiras in the enemy land – forts and entry points were left unarmed and *baloes* were left on the shores of Bicholim, Mahem, Piligao and other villages at the mercy of the enemies. The Portuguese men were accused of providing secret information and weapons to their lovers. These were later used by the enemies against the Portuguese.

The constant interference on the part of the Church authorities in non-religious matters was resented by the Viceroy Joao Saldanha da Gama. He complained to the Crown and to substantiate the complain, he enclosed his correspondence with the Parish Priests of S. Braz and S. Mathias (Ilhas). At one point the Archbishop had instigated Fr. Gabriel Silveira to complain to the Viceroy against one Dessay Ramogy Rao who was planning to celebrate Sigmo with *bailadeiras.*

II. HOMES FOR ORPHANS, WIDOWS AND DESTITUTES

At the turn of the sixteenth century and early seventeenth century three institutions were established in the city of Goa: *Recolhimento de Nossa Senhora da Serra, Recolhimento de Santa Maria Magdalena and Real Mosteiro da Santa Monica.* The first two were to shelter orphans and *arrependidas* respectively. The last one was a nunnery for pious women. These institutions were established largely due to the efforts of Archbishop Dom Aleixo de Menezes.

Recolhimento de Nossa Senhora da Serra (Retirement House of Our Lady of Mountain)

In the early centuries of the Portuguese rule, *orfas del Rei* from Portugal were regularly dispatched to India, to be married to Portuguese men working in the Estado da India. It was often difficult to find suitable accomodation with respectable families for these girls. Therefore, Dom Aleixo de Menezes, suggested a special home for the *orphans del Rei.*

Casa de Orfas was established in 1598 and it was housed temporarily in the Convent of Graça. In 1605, the home was shifted to new premises and named. *Recolhimento de Nossa Senhora da Serra* (BNL-Codice 176/F2527). The building was at the *Rua do Crucifixo* near the *Santa Casa da Misericordia de Goa* and the Church of *Nossa Senhora da Serra* (Our Lady of Mountain).

The administration of the Home was entrusted to *Santa Casa da Misericordia* – a charitable institution established in the first decade of the Portuguese rule. This institution protected orphans, supported honest widows, fed foundlings, redeemed captives, defended the prisoners, helped the needy, cured the poor sick and buried the dead indigent. In Goa, the Misericordia acted as executor of last will and testament, remitting the proceeds of a life time in the East to the families in other parts of the empire. The brotherhood managed also hospitals and other institutions.

The spiritual needs of the girls at the Serra were taken care by Augustinian Friars. The home was run by a *Regente* who was assisted by staff including a number of servants. The first Regente was D. Filipa Ferreira, a rich widow from *Praças do Norte* who later was appointed the first *Prioreza* (Superior) of the *Mosteiro de Santa Monica*

The Portuguese Crown provided for the upkeep of the *orfas del rei.* The State provided with 1% of its duties. Besides, the State among other things granted annually 100 *xerafins,* 20 *kandis* of rice and 10 *kandis* of wheat (AHU: India-Caixa 46/51). The institution was helped also by *Obras Pias* and *Misericordia.*

The Home was started exclusively for white Catholic women who were well born and between the ages of 14 to 30 years – they included *orfas del Rei* and girls of similar status whose fathers died in India due to diseases and wars. However, this clause was disregarded right from the beginning. In addition to *orfas* girls, the Home admitted respectable widows, wives, daughters and nieces of those men who had to leave Goa on expeditions or to fight wars of conquests. Wives abandoned by their husbands were also admitted as paying guests. In early years the Home housed about thirty girls.

Santa Casa da Misericordia de Goa had the responsibility of arranging suitable husbands for the orphan girls among the Portuguese men in the Estado da India. Orphan girls were given dowries at the time of marriage or when they joined a convent by the Crown, *Santa Casa da Misericordia, Senado* (Municipal Council) and from bequests left by people for such purpose. Husbands of orphan girls were given jobs and land. As for instances in the case of Ana Cornuvel and D. Catarina de

Souza. The former was given in 1631 as her dowry the village of Telery for three generation (HAG:CPA 1630-1631: 20v) and the latter when she married Antonio da Silva de Alte in 1644 was granted as dowry a *aforamento* at Douli for three generation and income derived from black dye from Baçaim (HAG:CPA liv 83:92). In 1667, the husband of one of the inmate Joana Ribeiro de Macedo was given the charge of Feitor of the city of Goa and charge of *armazens do mantimento. Santa Casa* of Cochin and others had also had similar responsibilities.

Since many of the *orphan girls* were given grants for three to four generations there was shortage of dowry for the new ones in form of land and posts for their husbands. In the mid seventeenth century due to high cost of living, the dowry of 1,000 *xerafins* was considered small. A few men came forward to marry orphan girls. As remarked earlier, many of these girls were neither so young nor good looking. In the second decade of the seventeenth century the institution was overcrowded with orphans girls waiting to be married wives and daughters of men who were fighting for the Crown. The situation forced the Archbishop of Goa to grant permission to house some of them at the Convent of Santa Monica (ANTT: DRI, liv.6/206). The waiting list for admission was also long.

Documents available of the seventeenth century show that contrary to existing rules the institution admitted women of doubtful virtue and illegitimate daughters. Apparently, the Viceroys pressurized *Santa Casa da Misericordia* to admit these *donzelas.* Many objected that women of doubtful virtue had to live with honest women. In 1615, the Portuguese Crown promulgated a strictly worded decree forbidding this practice. The decree was ignored and in 1634 the *Provedor and Irmaos* of the *Misericordia* were complaining to the Crown that women of doubtful character were still being admitted at the *Recolhimento de Nossa Senhora de Serra* (ANTT:DRI36). Consequently, a royal letter dated 1635 ordered the Viceroy to stop the practice(ANTT:DRI 33/234). The letter also reminded the Viceroy, that admission of *donzelas* in the Home was the prerogative of *Misericordia.* As in earlier instances, the contents of this letter were disregarded and Viceroys continued giving admission to *donzelas* at the *Serra.*

"Afilhadas" (Godchildren) of the Governors also were admitted in this home. Most of them were actually the illegitimate daughters of some of the Governors. Governors in India in the early period did not bring along their wives and some had mistresses in India. In 1688 a royal letter addressed to the *Mesa* (Board) of *Santa Casa da Misericordia* rebuked the institution for accepting girls born to Hindu, Muslim and African women.

The institution housed about 200 girls in 1679. The number of *orfas del Rei* began to decrease in the eighteenth century. In 1722 the Home had only 20 of these girls (AHU: India-Caixa 43/51). By this time few orphan girls came from Portugal. Majority of girls living in the home were *mestiças.*

Recolhimento da Serra continued to admit illegitimate girls. In 1729 the institution was banned again from accepting these girls. The number of the inmates increased during the fourth decade of the eighteenth century. This upswing may have been due to large number of girls continuing living in the home on account of inadequate dowry. Therefore, in 1735 the State decided to raise the dowry . In the early twentieth century each girl received as a *dote* a sum of Rs. 200.

In 1705, the Home was shifted from its originally premises to a larger place to accommodate about 150 girls and the staff. In 1836 the Home was again shifted to the Convent of S. Agostinho. By 1841 *Misericordia* could no longer maintain the huge old building of S.Agostinho, therefore, the institution was moved out of the city of Goa to the Carmelite Convent at Chimbel (suburb of Panjim). In addition, the city of Goa was very unhealthy place due to some endemic and epidemic diseases. Finally, in 1924, the home was shifted to Panjim. The building still exists and houses some *mestiço* women.

Recolhimento de Maria Magdalena

Regular complains that women of doubtful virtue were admitted in the same house as the orphan girls, forced Dom Aleixo de Menezes to start in 1611 *Recolhimento de Maria Magdalena* also known as *Casas das Penitentes, Arrependidas and Convertidas.* The home was established to shelter white women of easy life who had repented (HAG: Ms. 10421–EMM). It was started in a building near the College of St. Paul. Although it was originally established for white women only, in course of time the institution admitted also women of mixed blood. Preference was given to young and good looking – those who were likely to fall easily in trouble.

The girls were admitted on recommendation of their parents or the Parish Priest. Applicants were required to undergo medical check up to rule out the possibility of suffering from contagious diseases.

In case the inmate was well born and had a daughter below the age of eight years, she was permitted to have her in the home until the daughter completed 12 years after which the daughter was transferred to Serra (HAG: Ms. 10422-CCCSMM).

Adulterous women, women who had sufficient rent to maintain themselves, and women who were publicly punished by the State or the Church could not be admitted in the institution.

A special ceremony was performed when a woman was admitted in the home. She was received by a *regente, a porteira* and the inmates of the house all dressed in black. The new entrant was presented by the *Regente* with a veil of silk and a cross, which was received kneeling down. This was followed by singing of psalms and prayers. After the ceremony each inmate welcomed the new entrant with a hug. One of the inmates was appointed to familiarize the woman with the rules and practices of the house.

It was believed that confession was necessary for the well being of the girls. Therefore, every entrant had to confess to an elderly priest appointed for the purpose before she was entrusted with various tasks of the home. One of the regulation of the home advised the *Regente* not to press the girls for confessions and to give them sufficient time to make up their minds (HAG:Ms.10424 -ERSMM).

The rules of the home were very strict. The inmates had to wear white uniforms on Sundays and holydays, on other days they could wear the dress of the land with leather shoes. On special occasions they wore black. Talking was restricted to fixed time and that too on low voice. Unusual punishment were given to the guilty found visiting each other in the cubicles. Punishment included eating on the floor in the middle of the dining room or fasting three times a week.

Letters to the inmates were censored and those which might disturb the peace of the inmates were not delivered. Permission of their Superior had to be sought to write home. Visits were restricted to close relatives with prior permission of the *Regente*.(HAG: Ms. 10423-ERCC 1729). Visitors were received in the presence of the *regente* or a person appointed by her.

Recolhimento da Maria Magdalenã was also managed by *Santa Casa da Misericordia.* The members of the Board of Santa Casa visited the home twice a year, to inquire about the well being of the inmates. The members of the Board were required to seek permission from the *Provedor* to talk to the girls.

The day to day affairs of the home were looked after by a *Regente,* a woman of good character, who had to be at least forty years old and unmarried. During the later period widows were appointed as *Regente* but with a condition that these widows should not have grown up sons. The Regente was helped by a *porteira* (doorkeeper), two other women in addition to servants and slaves.

The home received in the seventeenth century an annual grant of 300 *xerafins.* In case the funds were not sufficient, two persons could be appointed to go around asking for alms. A record of the donations collected was kept in *Livro das Esmolas.*

Santa Casa da Misericordia de Goa had the responsibility of rehabiliting all those girls who had proved that they had repented. *Misericordia* tried reconciliation between married women living in the home and their estranged husbands and many times succeeded as in the case of Luiza Maria, wife of Manuel da Silva. Marriages were also arranged between the girls and men who were responsible for their disgrace. A small proportion of these girls from Goa eventually found their way on homebound ships to far away Portuguese colony of Brazil. Historical literature of the time also mentions that girls from this home were sent to Angola, Pegu, Malaca and other places.

A regulation issued in the second half of the eighteenth century, made provision to send out the so called *arrependidas and repentidas* from Goa to Ceylon. These girls were sent to marry Portuguese men at Ceylon (HAG:Ms.10424:3). The provision was made to prevent Portuguese men in Ceylon from marrying native girls. During this period similar girls were sent from mother country to Brazil, Angola and other places to marry Portuguese men there. Girls from Goa were sent at the care of *Santa Casa da Misericordia of Colombo.* Prior permission of the Viceroy was to be sought in order to send these women to Ceylon.

In 1705, the institution was moved from its original premises to a new place. From here it was in 1836 shifted to the Augustinian Convent. The Convent was vacant after the Augustinian friars had left it due to suppression of religious orders in Goa. In 1841 the institution along with *Recolhimento de Serra* was shifted to the Carmelite Convent at Chimbel.

Mosteiro de Santa Monica

Mosteiro de Santa Monica, an Augustinian Convent, was established in July 1606. The convent was one of the biggest of the Portuguese Empire, after the one at Odivelas (Portugal). The idea of establishing a convent for the girls was opposed right from the start by the clergy and secular authorities in Goa and at Portugal. They were of the opinion that such institution was not suitable for Indian girls owing to their great weakness and licentious upbringing (Boxer 1975). Several requests of the Archbishop were turned down by Viceroys. Finally, in early seventeenth century, the Portuguese Crown reluctantly granted permission to establish the convent. D. Martim Castro, the Viceroy of India had to live Goa to go to Malaca. In his absence Archbishop D. Aleixo de Menezes who was asked to take over the Government, decided to put the plan in practice.

Initially, the convent was set up in a temporary building and then moved to new premises close to the Augustinian monastery. The Convent still exists. *Mosteiro de Santa Monica* became well known within short span of time. Young girls from different parts of Asia and Portugal including the niece of V. Roy Ruy Lourenço de Tavora joined the institution.

The convent was started for girls of noble families, who lacked sufficient dowries to marry men of same social conditions (DRI MCMLXXIV:vi 121-122). It admitted also *novas cristas* (girls of Jewish origin), native women including illegitimate girls and newly converted Christians as for instance the two daughters of the ruler of Jafnapatan.

It started with 18 girls, one widow and two ladies in charge of the institution–D. Filipa Ferreira Sa who came to Goa from Tana and her daughter D. Maria Sa. D. Filipa was the wealthy widow of rich *Fidalgo* from Tana. Her household possessed over 200 slaves. She gave up her wealth to join the convent on the advice of frei Diogo Santa Ana. D. Filipa was appointed the first *Prioreza* of the Convent. In the first batch 16 girls made their vows, one died and one postponed her decision to take the vow. Majority of these girls were from Goa, a few were from Tana, Amboim and Malaca. Young girls from Portugal living at the *Recolhimento de Serra* also joined the Convent.

The girls when they joined the Convent, brought *dote* (dowry) along. The dowry was in cash and in kind. The dowry was meant for maintenance of the girls. Initially the dowry was 800 *xerafins* for Indian girls and 5 to 6 *xerafins* for white women (Santa Maria, 1699).

There were two kinds of nuns–nuns of *veo preto,* these were white women and nuns of *veo branco* were native Goans and a few from other parts of Asia. Discrimination was made between the nuns of *veo preto* and *nuns of veo branco*. Nuns of *veo preto* occupied important posts in the convent including the post of *Sorror* (superior).

In the early period the Convent faced several difficulties, particularly after the departure of D. Aleixo de Menezes to Portugal. The city of Goa had failed to help as promised to D. Aleixo de Menezes. Neither the institution was helped by the rich inhabitants except for D. Catharina de Mendonça who came to the rescue of the convent with large donations which helped the institution to carry on with the work (Santa Maria 1699: 156).

The Convent became famous within short period of time. C.R. Boxer remarks that "it became a kind of status symbol into which the best families of Goa tried to get one or more of their daughters accepted as novices". Large number of girls joined the convent in the seventeenth century. Girls joined the convent very early at the age of six. At this early age they were taught to read, write and sing. The noviciate started only after the girls had reached puberty. In the seventeenth century many wealthy girls preferred to join the convent rather than marry men of low moral character.

The orphans and other women from *Recolhimento de N. Sra de Serra* were many times sheltered at Santa Monica due to lack of accommodation in the former institution. This permission granted by the Archbishop of Goa was censured by the Archbishop of Lisboa.

During the second decade of the seventeenth century there were about 100 girls in the convent who carried large dowry. The convent had large *cabedal* (funds). This situation seemed to have disturbed the local authorities. In a letter dated 1620, Viceroy Fernao de Albuquerque was complaining to the Portuguese Crown about the shortage of eligible girls to marry and scarcity of funds to carry trade because the convent had stopped giving loans to the State. Did it really affect the trade.? This aspect needs further to be studied. One gets the impression that the Portuguese were more worried about not being able to maintain their white identity since many white girls joined the Convent, thus expoiling the chances of many bachelors who left the city. A parallel situation existed at Macau and Cochin during the same period. In one of his letter to the sovereign of Spain and Portugal, Dom Diogo Coutinho declares that "Cochin weeps for lack of its nobility".

The Viceroy Fernao Albuquerque requested his sovereign to reduce the number of admissions. Consequently, the number was reduced to 40 girls with a condition that the girls should be the ones of noble birth who lacked sufficient dowry to marry within the same social background (DRI,Tomo VIII).

Mosteiro of Santa Monica received income from villages it owned in different parts of Estado da India including Salcette (Baçaim). It received rent from several shops in Chorao, Divar and Jua (Ilhas). Some of these shops were rented to cloth merchants. In addition, income came in, from rent of several houses the convent owned at Rua Direita and other areas of the city of Goa. Some of these houses were gifted with stipulation that prayers and masses should be said for the dead (ANTT:DRI- liv 37). A large part of these houses and shops were part of dowry given to the nuns by their families and a few were bought by the convent. The convent also had several rice fields including the ones in Bardez. The convent on many occasions played the role of money lender, lending substantial sums to private traders but on some occasions refused the same to the State on the plea of poverty.

The convent continued to admit large number of girls contrary to the orders issued by the State. D. Miguel de Noronha, Conde de Linhares, in an entry in his diary dated 1632 ,mentions about a letter sent by the inhabitants of the city of Goa. In this letter they explained the problems created by large number of girls joining the convent with large dowries. The city was deserted by the nobles because they could not find girls to marry of their nobility. Conde de Linhares requested the Crown to reduce the size and to fix the amount of dowry each girl could carry. During this period vast land in the city belonged to the convent. Consequently, the Crown limited the number to 100 girls. New novices could not be admitted unless to make up the number. A document signed between the Superior of the convent and the city Municipality permitted each girl to bring only 1,000 *xerafins* as dowry . To compensate for lack of dowry, the Government decided to grant 8000 *xerafins* to the convent. The Portuguese Crown accepted the Padroado of Santa Monica in 1636 (ANTT:DRI 37:381). The convent was renamed at this time as *Real Convento de Santa Monica.*

Sixty years later, in 1697 the Superior of the convent was complaining about the failure of the Government to release the grant of 8000 *cruzados.* In the same petition she was complaining about the high cost of victuals such as rice, wheat, vegetables, butter, oil, fire-wood, meat, and fish, and the need to raise the subsidy to 16000 *cruzados* (AHU: India-Caixa 39/4).

The nuns of Santa Monica lived a simple life, cut their hair short and wore a habit. They took four vows – poverty, obedience, chastity and cloister. Despite the vow of cloister, the nuns of Santa Monica left the convent at three occasions. Twice with the permission of the Archbishop and once without his permission. They left for the first time in 1636 when the convent caught fire on Christmas eve. They were sheltered for a year in the Augustinian Convent in the city of Goa. The second time they left the institution when some of them revolted against the Church authorities and the third time they went to Mormugao due to Maratha invasion.

The nuns of Santa Monica were not above the Church politics. In 1731 they revolted against the Church authorities. The revolt started as a result of conflicts between some Goan clergy supported by the Bishop of Malaca and the Archbishop of Goa (Church Review 1992:ii). The Superior of the convent and some nuns supported the former, while the sub-prioress Ignacia de Anunciaçao together with remaining nuns supported the later.

Those who opposed the Archbishop were threatened that they would be sent on exile to far away places such as Macau. On account of the threat the nuns left the convent supported by Jesuits and Augustinian priests. They sought shelter elsewhere in the city. Nevertheless, they were persuaded to return back to the convent within short period of time.

In May 1732 the opposing nuns led by their Prioress left the convent once more, when they came to know about the visit of the Archbishop of Goa to the convent. This time they sought shelter in the old palace of the Viceroys, situated near the Arch of Viceroys in the city of Goa. The nuns stayed there for six months. In 1738, Viceroy Conde de Sandomil prevailed on the nuns to return to the convent. The conflict was settled when the Archbishop promised to accept certain demands made by the rebel nuns. The rebel nuns in their turn promised submission to the Archbishop. In the same year a new Prioress was elected for the convent from among the rebel nuns (the Prioress was elected every three years).

Discrimination continued to be a problem in the convent throughout the period. A royal order dated 1779 tried to end this discrimination (HAG: Ms.159B -MR :558). The nuns of *veu branco* were advised to wear *veu preto*. In the nineteenth century the white nuns paid on admission Rs. 100 and native ones double of this amount. The convent received from the State an annual grant of Rs. 1000.

The convent of Santa Monica began to loose its importance with the decay of the city of Goa. In 1804 the convent had 61 nuns and 4 novices. This number came down to 30 in 1827 and further decreased to 8 nuns in 1834 when it decided not to take novices. Majority of nuns during the nineteenth century were natives. After 1855 the number was reduced to 4 nuns. The last nun to die in this institution was Soror Maria do Espirito

Santo from Cavelossim (Goa). During its 276 years of existence about 661 nuns took vows in this convent.

A Day in the Life of a Monica

The daily routine for the nuns at the Mosteiro of Santa Monica was well organized. The day began very early at 3 a.m with one hour of prayers, followed by plain tea. After the tea and until the mass, the nuns were busy taking care of their personal needs. The mass was held in the convent chapel at 7 o'clock. When this mass was over, the nuns occupied themselves with studies or with various tasks assigned to them such as preparing articles of handicrafts, rosaries, purses, confectioneries, sweets such as *doce bagi* and *dedos de damas.* This was a rare delicacy, the recipe of which was a well guarded secret with the nuns.

Lunch at noon consisted of rice and curry. Twice a week they eat fish and sometimes meat. Special food was cooked on the feast day of Santa Monica, Santo Agostinho, Santo Antonio, Christmas and Easter. The meals were prepared by female cooks with a number of helpers. This staff was entitled to 20 measures of rice. They too had to rise very early and they were taught the Christian doctrine by the nun entrusted to look after them.

After lunch and until 2 o'clock a complete silence was maintained, work not even in the kitchen was carried out. The servants retired to their respective quarters leaving the nuns alone. At 2 o'clock the bell rang for a two hour prayers. When the prayers were over and until the Angeles the nuns went for a stroll in the beautiful garden to breath fresh air before retiring to their rooms. They met again at the Chapel for prayers.

Dinner was served at 8 o'clock. Dinner was followed by community meeting, expect the day they received the Eucharist. The nuns confessed and received the Eucharist as a rule twice a week and on feast days. They fasted twice a week and more often during the lent and advent.

The nuns were not permitted to speak privately with the other members of the community besides their superiors. No outsiders above 6 years except for a doctor or a priest in case of illness were permitted in the cell, that too in the presence of the Superior who stood at some distance. The cells were simple with a bed, a cross on the wall or a statue of Virgin Mary, and a cattle containing holy water.

Each nun was paid seventy seven *xerafins* of copper annually for their maintenance. In case they. occupied a post they were paid an allowance of 44 *xerafins.* In addition, they were given seven and half kandis of unhusked rice, eleven hands of wheat, seventy-five *xerafins* for clothes, forty *xerafins* for expenses on a feast day and for non-specified expenses seventy-five *xerafins*. The congregation looked after the medical and some other expenses of the nuns and salaries of the servants.

Visitors were permitted once a month, except during the time of advent, lent, Sundays and holydays. Visits were, however, restricted to parents, siblings and immediate members of the family. They could speak only through a small *locutorio* (nuns called it purgatory) in the presence of another nun. Prior permission of the Superior had to be sought to write home. These letters were censored by the Superior. Probably, to check these nuns who wrote to their family about the life in the convent.

Other Institutions for Women in Twentieth Century

In the twentieth century the Church in Goa established some more institutions to provide shelter to destitute women, unwed mothers, illegitimate children and orphan girls. Among these institutions there are two well-known institutions:

Lar da Santa Terezinha, Margao

The home started in 1944 due to initiative of Frei Maria Jose OCD at Margao, provided shelter to young orphan and destitute girls. The institution was run with the help of donations and income derived from cottage industry started by the institution (AAGD 1955:47).

Obra de Proteçao a Mulher

This institution was established in 1947 at Birondem (Satari taluka) by Fr. Amaro Pinto Lobo from Tivim. Obra de Proteçao a Mulher provided shelter to destitute women, unwed mothers, orphans and illegitimate children. The home was under the *Obra Diocesana de Protecçao a Mulher.* It was managed by Freiras Franciscanas Portuguesas. In 1954 the institution was moved to Panjim.

III. WOMEN'S EDUCATION

Generally, the Church did not promote women's education in Goa until perhaps the fag end of the Portuguese rule in Goa. However, there was one exception – the nuns of Santa Monica – they were provided education from the time of its inception in the seventeenth century. Apparently, the Church did not feel the need to promote the education of women in Goa although generally it tried to uplift her conditions.

A pastoral letter dated 1745 issued by Archbishop Dom Lourenço de Santa Maria decreed that both men and women could not marry unless they could speak Portuguese but in practice no measures were adopted to implement the decree.

In a circular dated July 1895 the Church banned girls from attending Parochial schools and advised the Parish priests to explain to the parents disadvantages of sending their daughters to schools meant for both sexes.

Instituto de N. Sra de Piedade

Irmas Hospitaleiras were in charge of *Colegio de Nossa Senhora de Piedade* for girls. This institution was closed down in early twentieth century and replaced by a *Escola Nacional do Sexo Feminino*. In 1952 the institute was renamed as *Instituto de N. Sra. de Piedade* and handed over by the State to the Goa Diocese. The nuns of *Sociedade das Filhas do Coraçao de Maria* were asked by the Archbishop to run this institute for girls. It had a total 137 students. The institution provide education to girls in Home Sciences.

In the last decades of the Portuguese rule in Goa there were some schools run by the nuns where young girls were imparted education in English upto High School. These convent schools were attached to educational boards in other parts of India.

This chapter has focussed on attempts made by the Church to provide better conditions for women in Goa during the Portuguese colonial rule. It issued decrees to correct some of the negative aspects of our culture – it worked to promote widow remarriages and end tonsuring of widows, polygamy and child marriages. The Church, on many occasions tried to influence the State to issue decrees in order to give women better status in the society. The property and other rights granted to widows and orphan girls in Goa were due to the efforts of the Church. In some occasions the Church did not succeed in its attempts to influence the State probably because the State was reluctant to interfere with the customs and traditions of the people or lack of interest on the part of the Government.

The Church throughout the Portuguese rule was concerned with the activities of *bailadeiras* and prostitutes. Several times it drew the attention of the State about the problem. This resulted in some well-known alvaras issued by the State.

The Church established institutions to shelter destitute women and orphan girls but it failed to promote women's education in Goa.

6

OVERVIEW

The year 1998 will mark the quincentenary of the Portuguese arrival in India. In this context an attempt has been made to study the status of women in Goa during the colonial rule and to assess the impact of this rule on the conditions of women in Goa – an old colony of Portugal in the west coast of India.

When the Portuguese arrived in this land, women in Goa as in other parts of the globe were dominated by men. The birth of a daughter was not always welcome. However, so far no documentation has been found to prove the existence of infanticide in Goa, that is deliberate killing of girl child such the one that was practiced among some tribes in other parts of India.

Pre-puberty marriages were common in Goa. Seclusion, polygamy and sati prevailed in the society. Widow remarriages were not permitted. Women had no property rights. Customs, traditions and religion including folk religion had its sway on the life of Goan women. Customs and traditions encouraged women to play several traditional roles of a daughter, wife, mother and daughter-in-law. While others imposed taboos on them and kept women dependent on men. Some of these customs restricted women's freedom and hindered their self-development. Women were – the subservient ones.

Immediately after the Conquest of Goa, Afonso de Albuquerque, initiated his well-known mixed marriage policy between his country men in India and native women. The purpose was to create a white identity in the Estado da India and to have a community that would be loyal to the Portuguese rulers. Elsewhere in India, the British during their rule discouraged their men even from marrying Anglo-Indian girls. *Politica dos Casamentos* was one of the first policy adopted by the new rulers which had an impact on a section of women in Goan society. It resulted in the union of the two races and mingling of eastern and western cultures. As a result women who married Portuguese men converted to new religion and could at once claim all the privileges of a born Portuguese. They learnt to speak the Portuguese language and many of their customs and manners. While some women married to Portuguese whites continued to follow their earlier customs, traditions and folk religion.

The Portuguese men in the early period, for reasons already mentioned, migrated to India without their wives. This had a significant implication in the life style of Goan women. Native women were involved in all kinds of relationships with the Portuguese men.

The Portuguese rule made a difference on the status of women in Goa. During the 450 years of their rule a considerable volume of legislations concerning women were enacted in Goa by the Portuguese rulers. Many of these laws were enlightened ones and some of these were meant to prevent gender discrimination. The reforms brought to Goan women the benefits of justice. Christian women were first to benefit from the reforms granted to women by the new rulers. Hindu women specially from New Conquests, were for long time governed by their *Codigo dos Usos e Costumes.* However, by the end of the nineteenth century Hindu women were permitted to opt out of their Hindu Law and seek justice under Portuguese law.

Women in the Goan society enjoyed several rights much before their counterparts elsewhere in India. For instance, as early as the sixteenth century women in Goa were granted the right to inherit property of their husbands and fathers in the absence of sons.

Generally, the Portuguese were concerned about the upliftment of women in Portuguese India . Reforms were introduced to do away with some negative practices existing in our society such as sati, child marriages, tonsuring of widows and polygamy. *Sati,* which was abolished soon after the conquest of Goa, was a founding legislation in the history of women in Goa. Albuquerque abolished a practice which probably appeared to him to be barbaric.

Tonsuring of the widows was also banned from early times, but non-Christian women in Goa continued with the practice until last few decades of the colonial rule. A few women took advantage of the law that permitted widow remarriage. Probably because the prejudice against the widow was so deep-rooted in our society, that the legislation had no effect. In addition, few men came forward to marry them due to stigma attached to widows by customs and traditions. It was difficult to arrange husbands for widows.

Another negative practice in the Goan society was polygamy. This practice was prohibited in 1567, despite the prohibition the practice persisted. Hindu men were permitted by their *Codigo dos Usos e Costumes* to have more than one wife. Since the State did not succeed in abolishing polygamy, it tried to control polygamy. Man desirous of contracting a second marriage had to seek a prior written permission of his previous wife and the State. Usually first wives refused to grant this permission and often pressure had to exerted to get the same. While a non-Christian man could have another wife according to their customs and usages, a Goan woman could not even opt out of an unhappy or undesirable marriage until 1910. There were double standards in these matters.

There are instances when apparently conversion was the motive behind some of the measures, which were designed to favour the promotion of Christianity. This was more true in the earlier centuries of the Portuguese rule – economic incentives were provided to persuade women to convert to Christianity. Sops for conversion were granted in case of property rights. In the early years, Hindu widows and orphans were not entitled to property of their dead husbands and fathers, unless they converted to Christianity.

The Portuguese Civil Code, 1867 brought further benefits to women in Goa. The Code is still in force in Goa, eventhough it has been replaced in Portugal in 1967. The Portuguese Civil Code introduced several changes including the one that guaranteed equality of sexes in respect of inheritence of property. On the death of the head of the family automatically one half of his property would go to the wife and the remaining half of the property was diyided equally among his children irrespective of sex. In the rest of India daughters had no right to the family property until 1956 but only to *streedan*. *Streedan* consisted of dowry in form of jewellery and personal possession which was given to a daughter at the time of her marriage.

As mentioned earlier, although daughters were granted property rights by law, fathers and brothers found ways and means to deny married daughters and sisters of their rights, on the grounds that they were given dowry at the time of marriage. This was done to prevent division of the family property. Actually dowry in cash given by upper class Goan families to their daughters at the time of marriage was a kind of advance to what they were actually entitled on the death of their parents. Girls at time of marriage were asked to sign *disistencia* on the grounds that they were given dowry. Legally *disistencia* was valid only if it was given after the death of the father and not earlier. At times, daughters were given much less than what they were entitled to by law. Among the upper classes it was a tradition to keep some daughters unmarried at home, so that the family property remained undivided for the son.

Wealthy families also sometimes found ways of depriving their daughters-in-law of the family property by making them sign an pre-nuptial contract whereby they agreed to forego their claim to half of the property of the husband. The motive was to keep the wealth within the family of the husband.

The code raised the age of marriage for girls and boys. This was an important measure to end early marriages prevalent in the Goan society of the time. But child marriages continued in Goa until the twentieth century. In fact, some backward classes of *Kunbis, potters* and *scavengers* were permitted to get their daughters married at 12 years and sons at 14 years of age as per the legislation of 1928.

The constitutional changes of 1910 in Portugal resulted in further benefits for women. Divorce was permitted for the first time to the inhabitants of Portugal and her colonies. Women had now the right to terminate an undesirable marriage. The number of women who availed themselves of this law was very small. Socio-religious taboos prevented women from resorting to divorce. In addition, the economic factor must have also played a role. Women in Goa, in those days were not economically independent. Majority of women, being uneducated, were unaware about the legislation. Even today, most women – whether they are educated or uneducated prefer to suffer rather than opt out of an incompatible marriage because of social stigma attached to divorce.

Legally, the position of women in Goa during the colonial period was considerably upgraded. Notwithstanding extensive reforms issued to improve the conditions of women, we have seen from the historical literature of the time that in practice women did not avail themselves of these legislation. Socio-religious factors prevented women from taking advantage of the legislation introduced by the rulers. At other times the laws enacted by the rulers were not effectively implemented. The colonial Government appears to have been reluctant to impose strictly measures against some customs in the Goan society, possibly because it feared might offended the feelings of the inhabitants, provoke resentment or even revolt as for instance in the case of widow remarriage and sati. In fact, in mid sixteenth century, the ban on sati was temporarily lifted by the State as a result of petitions and pressures from the people. However, it was reinforced soon after but not strictly until 1884.

The State made unsuccessful attempts through out the period under review to ban the activities of prostitutes and *bailádeiras*. As in the case of other reforms, measures against prostitutes and *bailadeiras* were not strictly implemented. The authorities were accused of turning a blind eye to such activities and even of associating with them. Prostitution was responsible for large scale spread of venereal disease in the city of Goa and other places. While the State tried to curb prostitution, it failed to introduce measures to improve the conditions of the slaves and end slave trade until the second half of the nineteenth century.

Majority of the women were not formally educated. The education of women was neglected. The attitude of the State, Church and society in general were responsible for this state of affairs. Apparently, it did not suit a patriarchal society of the time to provide education for women. Women were not expected to work in the milieu of men. A woman's only purpose in life was the bearing and rearing of children. Education was made available for women only during the last 60 years of the Portuguese rule in Goa.

Education benefited a small section of women, mainly from the Old Conquests. Education of women in the New Conquests territories, which were predominantly non-Christian, was completely neglected. At times many parents influenced by customs and traditions refused to send their young daughters to school. Some girls of upper strata were provided education at home with the help of male tutors.

In the early decades of the twentieth century the society was made aware through the media and other agencies about the need to educate women. Lack of education affected women's self development, culture and upbringing of the children.

Yet, there were women who distinguished themselves in the last 50 years of the Portuguese rule in the field of nursing, teaching, creative writing, music and politics. Many of them have shown extraordinary courage and capacity in bringing up their children single handedly, in case of the death of the husband or his absence from Goa. Poor economic conditions compelled many poor and middle class men to migrate in large number from the end of the nineteenth century. They left Goa every year for better prospects to British India and Africa. Majority of the wives stayed back, and did not accompany their husbands in far away places. They stayed back to care for the old in-laws and raise their children. Those few who accompanied their husbands to Africa and other places, returned, when the children reached school going age, so as to provide them with formal western kind of education.

In a typical Goan household of the lower strata there was a division of labour. The men undertook repair of the house, marketing besides their main "occupation", while the wife cooked, performed several household tasks and some helped the husbands in agricultural work. In the absence of the migrated husband the work load of the wife increased. However, there was little change in the authority structure of the family. Major decisions were in most cases postponed until the absent partner could return home.

Unmarried Goan women, widows and a few married women also migrated on their own to British India for better prospectus or further studies. A significant number of Goan women settled in the cosmopolitan city of Bombay. Feminine emigration was predominantly restricted to women of lower strata. They stayed away for certain length of time. Women worked in offices, schools, hospitals, factories or as maids in the homes of British and Parsi families.

Goan women, who migrated to British India, sent regular remittances back home to Goa which helped to raise the standard of living of their families. Remittances were also invested in jewellery, land and houses. Life for emigrant women was not easy. They had to face great hardships and make many sacrifices. Several factors led them to involve in immoral lives in the big cities.

The Church in Goa played a significant role to improve the status of women, whatever her motives might have been. The Church was responsible in introducing a new culture that was evolved in the West. This culture had an impact in the life style of women and mainly the Christian women in Goa.

The Church in Goa was concerned towards the plight of women who were oppressed and ill treated by their husbands, families and the society. She issued decrees to uplift the conditions of women. The Church in Goa was a powerful institution who could influence the Government in important matters. On many occasions, the State embodied suggestions made by the Church to grant benefits for Goan women. This resulted in many far sighted legislations including the encouragement of widow remarriages, property rights to widows and orphan girls and ban on polygamy. The Church also showed concern towards the poor slaves and female slaves in particular. It tried to give them a better deal in the hands of their masters.

Wars, conquests and diseases had taken a heavy toll of life, leaving behind orphans and widows. In addition, the lax sexual morality of the sixteenth century society in Goa, had created problems for women. To help and shelter these women the Church established homes at the end of the sixteenth and early seventeenth centuries. Initially the homes were started to help white women, but in course of time these homes provided shelter to mestiço women as well.

In the early seventeenth century the Church started a nunnery in the city of Goa where many well to do families tried to get admission for their daughters – having a nun in the family being a matter of prestige.

Women benefited and suffered due to various decrees issued by the Church. Women suffered at the hands of the Holy Inquisition. The Holy Inquisition imposed wide ranging prohibitions against practices which were considered to be signs of non-Christian influence. Among these, were the bans that prevented Christian women from wearing cholis and nosestuds. Reforms and decrees issued by the Church and Holy Inquisition at time alienated Goan women from their existing culture. After all that has been said, the Church did inject a dose of modernity in the life of Goan women.

Patriarchy continued to be strong in Goa as elsewhere in Asia. Today, women have come a long way. The position of women has improved considerably over the last few decades.

Education has made women conscious of their rights. The literacy rate in Goa is quite high. Primary education is compulsory and free, upto secondary school level for girls. Having taken advantage of equal education, women today want to demonstrate their caliber. They have made progress in many fields. Spheres of activity are widening, most specially for women who live in urban areas. Women in urban areas in Goa are slowly making inroads. They are making claims in decision making. Women are beginning to get organized. Women today are in many professions; including medicine, engineering, teaching, business management, politics and even defense forces. We had a woman Chief Minister and some legislators too but their number is very small.

In the last thirty years Goan women have migrated to many parts of the globe. Some to accompany their husbands, while others on their own. A large number of these women have migrated to the Arab countries on their own. Women who migrate, continue to be predominantly of lower strata of the society who work there as domestic servants. Women of middle and higher strata have also started migrating to these countries to be with their husbands. Many of them, in course of time, have taken jobs.

Goan women migrate to improve their standard of living as well as of their families. These women are contributing towards the Goan economy. In the middle Eastern countries women often undergo great hardships and are exploited by their masters. Feminine emigration specially emigration of married women, has had its impact on the family.

The educated section of women in Goa enjoy hitherto undreamed economic independence. But economic independence alone will not solve the many problems facing women. Discriminatory attitudes are deeply entrenched, and boys are still valued much more highly than girls.

Although women are as highly qualified as men and many times have done better than men in the educational field, yet very few women occupy important posts in the Government, educational institutions, industrial fields or are members of the state legislature. Discrimination against women continues. Majority of the men resent women in higher positions. They resent assertive women with a mind of their own. Most women, as in many parts of the world, continue to be excluded from decision -making process. The exclusion is spread to all levels–Government, corporate, social and household. Women are expected by a male dominated society to depend on men for important decisions.

Working women, not only supplement family income, but shoulder domestic responsibility in disproportionate amounts. Few men help their wives in the household work. They expect women to attend to them.

Overwhelming majority of women in Goa live in the rural areas, where the situation is infinitely worse. The conditions of rural women have not changed much over the years. Women in rural areas carry on traditional roles and adhere to norms which have come down from generation to generation. Even in urban areas traditional roles and values relating to women find wide acceptance.

Torture and harassment of women still continue even among some educated people. Dowry deaths, wife beating and other discriminations against women exist. The legal rights that she enjoys have not affected the old attitudes. The old attitudes still persist. Basic injustice still exists in the life of Goan women. Women are still held back by the forces of poverty, history, customs and traditions.

DOCUMENTARY APPENDICES

APPENDIX-1

Taluka-wise Literacy Rate Among Women in 1910

Talukas	Read and write
Ilhas	3051
Salcete	4204
Bardez	7019
Pernem	318
Sanquelim	417
Satari	50
Ponda	705
Sanguem	230
Quepem	209
Canacona	134

Census 1910

APPENDIX-2

Instructions issued by the Church in the Province of Mormugao to improve the Moral Conditions of Women.

In 1771, the Church inquiry committee accused Luisa of sudra class, widow of Ventura Gonsalves, living near the Church of aborting her foetus through violent methods. She was asked to explain her action and ordered to be imprisoned.

Flomazia and Maria both married living in the Church ward, daughters of late Gabriel along with their mother were accused of soliciting in public. They were ordered by the Church committee to be imprisoned.

Esperança, unmarried daughter of Antonia (widow of late Domingos de Araujo), living in the property of P. Ignacio Coelho was accused of getting pregnant twice with knowledge of her mother. Both were punished with imprisonment.

Further, the Church inquiry committee found out that Esperança widow of Estevao and her daughter were involved in prostitution. As a punishment they were ordered to be imprisoned.

Source: PP: *Visitas Pastoral*, vols. 11-12, fl. 20.

APPENDIX-3

Ban on Practices at the Time of Marriage

The Church in Goa directly or through its agency imposed ban on certain practices followed at the time of marriage by Christian women. The ban was imposed to prevent these women from following *costumes gentilicos* (non-Christian customs) prevailing in Goa.

The Fifth Church Council ordered that the father of the bride should not wash the feet of the daughter and son-in-law soon after the wedding ceremony, as it was a practice followed by *gentios*.

The Christian brides of Salcete followed a Hindu custom of taking with them a piece of jewellery to be worn after the Church wedding. The episcopal decree of July 1644 banned such custom. The same decree banned women from wearing nose ring.

A decree issued by the Goa Inquisition dated 14th April, 1736 banned Christian brides from being massaged with turmeric, coconut oil, coconut juice, flour and other things on the eve of marriage as was done by Muslim and Hindu women. It banned the practice of carrying betel and arecanut along with dowry. Women were banned from singing *vovios* at the time of marriage.

Native Christian women, specially of lower strata, followed another non-Christian custom of covering their face at the time of the wedding. The Church did away with the practice. In 1780 priests were instructed not allow brides to cover their faces as was being done by non-Christian brides. Priests failing to follow the order were to be suspended from their jobs in the Parish.

Christian brides were banned from wearing clothes and jewellery sent from the house of the groom soon after the Church wedding since it was a non-Christian custom.

Source: ANTT: *Conselho Geral do Santo Oficio: Inquisiçao de Goa,* Maço 36, no. 23.

APPENDIX-4

List of Women Accused, Imprisoned and Punished by the Holy Inquisition in the 18th Century

Catharina, alias Boteli, widow of Joao de Souza, midwife from Nerul (Bardez) for resorting to non-Christian superstitions at the time of deliveries. As a punishment she was forbidden to practice her trade.

Anna Pinto, widow of Bento Passanha, midwife from Chinchinim (Salcete) for attributing the cause of illness of a child to evil spirits and for advising superstitious cure. She was exiled for two years to the garrison area of Rachol.

Anna Maria Telles, wife of Francisco Valladares, for resorting to superstitious rituals as a cure for her illness. She was imposed spiritual penance.

Luiza Fernandes, alias Sobolem, widow of Paulo Fernandes, fishermen from S. Lourenço de Linhares (Sinquerim) Bardez, for performing non-Christian rituals at a marriage. She was granted spiritual penance.

Maria Fernandes, married to Andre Fernandes, from Parra Bardez was accused of resorting to non-Christian rituals including ancestor worship for the success of a marriage and a delivery. She was given spiritual penance.

Ana Afonso and Catharina Roiz of S. Lourenço de Linhares were accused by the Holy Inquisition of following non-Christian practices on the eve of their wedding.

Source: ANTT: *Conselho Geral do Santo Oficio: Inquisiçao de Goa, Maço 33 no. 24.*

BIBLIOGRAPHY

Archival Sources

Historical Archives of Goa

Estatutos de Maria Magdalena, 1605.

Copia dos Estatutos de Maria Magdalena — Estatuos de casa das Penintes e Convertida desta Cidade feitas pelo Dom Aleixo Menezez.

Estatutos do Recolhimento das Convertidas, 1729.

Estatutos de Santa Maria Magdalena, 1765.

Estatutos de Maria Madalena, 1765.

Livro das Provisoes e Alvaras da Santa Casa Misericordia de Goa.

Livro do Registo das Cartas do Reino.

Monçoes do Reino.(1560-1914).

Misericordia de Goa — Orfas e escravas 1780-1783.

Provisoes a favor de Cristandade.

Relaçao de Goa — Livros Vermelhos.

Arquivo do Palacio Patriarcal, Panjim

Visitas Pastorais, 1747-1927.

Arquivo National da Torre de Tombo

Conselho Geral do Santo Oficio (Inquisiçao de Goa).

Ordenaçoes do Reino.

Documentos Remetidos da India.

Arquivo da Santa Casa Misericordia de Lisboa

Various loose documents concerning Santa Casa Misericordia de Goa.

Arquivo Historico Ultramarino - Lisboa

Caixas da India.

Biblioteca National de Lisboa (Reservados)

Collecçao Pombalina.

1. Published Sources

Abreu, Miguel Vicente, *Real Mosteiro de Santa Monica de Goa — Memoria Historica* , Nova Goa, Imprensa National, 1882.

Albuquerque, Afonso de, *Cartas para el rei D. Manuel I,* ed. Antonio Baiao, Lisboa, Livraria Sa da Costa, 1942.

–, –,*Cartas, seguidas de documentos que as elucidam,* ed. Raymundo A. Bulha~o Pato, 6 vols. Lisboa, Academia Real das Sciencias, 1884-1915.

Albuquerque, Bras, *Commentarios do Grande Afonso Dalboquerque,* 5th ediçao, Tomo II, Partes III and IV, Lisboa, Imprensa National, 1973.

Altekar, A.S., *The Position of Women in Hindu Civilization,* 3rd edtion, Delhi, Motilal Banarsidass, 1962.

A Mulher Pobre na Historia da Igreja Latino – Americana, S. Paulo, ediçoes Paulinas, 1984.

Asian and Pacific Women's Resources and Action series —Health, Kuala Lampur, Asian and Pacific Development Centre, 1989.

Archivo Portuguez – Oriental, ed., J.H. da Cunha Rivara, 10 vols, Nova Goa, Imprensa Nacional, 1857-1876.

Arquivo Portugues Oriental, ed., A.B. de Bragança Pereira, 11 vols, Bastora, Tipografia Rangel, 1936-1940.

Azevedo, Alves de, *No paiz do faquir e da miseria,* Lisboa, 1957.

Ballhatchet, K., *Race, Sex and Class under the Raj,* New Delhi, Vikas Publishing House, 1969.

Balsemao, E.A. de Sa Nogueiro Pinto, *Os Portugueses no Oreinte,* Nova Goa, 1881.

Banerji, Sures Chandra and Ramala, *The Castaway of Indian Society,* Calcutta, Punthi Pustak, 1989.

Baioo, A. *A Inquisiça~o de Goa,*2 vols., Coimbra,1930-1945.

Barreto Miranda, J.C., *Quadros Historicos de Goa,* III, Margao, Tipografia Ultramar, 1865.

Barreto Miranda, Roque B., *Enfiada de Anexins Goeses.*

Barros, Joao de, *Decadas da Asia,* 4 vols, Lisboa, na regia Officina Typografia, 1777-1778.

Bocarro, A., *Livro das Plantas de todos as Fortalezas Cidades e povoaçaes do estado da India oriental,* in A. B. de Bragança Pereira (ed.), *Arquivo Portugues Oriental,* vol III, Bastora, Tipografia Rangel, 1936-1940.

Boletim Ofical, Nova Goa, Imprensa Nacional, 1880-1961.

Boletim de Filmoteca Ultramarina Portuguesa, Lisboa, Centro do Estudos Historicos Ultramarino, 1954-71.

Bose, M.L., *A Social and Cultural History of Ancient India* .

Bordalo, Francisco Maria, *Ensaio sobre a Estatisca do Estado Da India,* in Jose Joaquim Lopes de Lima, *Ensaios sobre a Estatisca das Possesoes Portuguesas na Africa, Asia, e na Oceania,* Lisboa, Imprensa Nacional, 1884-1862.

Botelho de Souza, Alfredo, *Subsidios para Historia Militar e Maritima da India, 4 vols, Lisboa, Agencia Geral das Colonias, 1940.*

Bouchon, Genevieve, *L'Asie du sud a l'epoque des Grandes Decouvertes,* London, Variorum Reprint, 1987.

Boxer, C.R., "*Fidalgos Portugueses e Bailadeiras Indianas (Seculos XVII e XVIII),*" Revista de Historia, Universidade de Sao Paulo, Departamento de Historia, 1961.

–, –, *Race Relations in the Portuguese Colonial Empire, 1415-1825,* London, Oxford University Press, 1963.

–, –, *The Portuguese Seaborne Empire, 1415-1825,* Middlesex, Penguin Books, 1973.

–, –, *Mary and Misogyny: Women in the Iberian Expansion Overseas - Some facts, fancies and personality, 1415-1815,* London, G. Duckworth and Co, 1975.

–, –, *Portuguese India in mid seventeenth century,* New Delhi, Oxford University Press, 1980.

–, –, *Fidalgos no Extremo Oriente,* Macau, Tipografia Macau Hung Heng, 1990.

–, –, *Casados e Cobatogem in the Estado da India, 16th and 17th centuries,*II International Seminar on Indo-Portuguese, ed. L. de Albuquerque and I. Guerreiro, Lisboa, *Centro da Historia e Cartografia Antiga,* 1985.

Bumiller, Elisabeth, *May You Be The Mother of Hundred Sons,* New Delhi, Penguin Books, 1992.

Bragança Pereira, *Etnografia da India Portuguesa,* 2 vols, Bastora, Tipografia Rangel, 1940.

Bridging Worlds — Studies on Women in south Asia, ed. Sally J.M. Sutherland, Delhi, Oxford University Press, 1992.

Brion, Hypacio de, *A India Portuguesa,* Lisboa, 1908.

Bullarium Patronatus in ecclesis Africae, Asiae atque Oceaniae, ed. V. de Paiva Manso, 3 vols, Lisboa, Typographia Nacional, 1872.

Burton, Richard F., *Goa and the Blue Mountains,* New Delhi, Asian Educational Services, 1991 (Reprint).

Carre, Abbe, *The Travels of the Abbe Carre in India and the near East, 1672-74*, 3 vols, London, 1947-48.

Census do Estado da India, 1881-1960.

Chandra, Sudhir, "Conflicted Beliefs and Men's Consciousness about women: Widow marriage in late nineteenth century Indian literature", *Economic and Political Weekly* (EPW), XXII, no. 44, 31 October, 1987.

"Challenge of Women's Studies", *EPW,* XVI, n. 27, 4 July, 1981, pp. 1163-1164.

Chattopadhyaya, Kamaladevi, *Indian women's Battle for Freedom*, New Delhi, Abhinav Publication, 1983.

Chowdhry, Prem,"Socio-Economic Dimension of Certain Customs and Attitudes: Women In Haryana in the colonial period" *EPW,* XXII, no. 48, 28 Nov. 1987.

Chen, Marty, "Poverty, Gender, and Work in Bangladesh", *EPW,* XXI, n. 5, 1 February,1986, pp. 217 - 222.

Codigo Civil Portugues, ed. Fernando Andrade P. de Lima and Joao de matos A. Varela, Coimbra, Coimbra Editora Limitada, 1956.

Collecçao da Legislaçao Novissima do Ultramar.

Conde de Linhares, *Diario do 3º Conde de Linhares*, 2 vols, Lisboa, Biblioteca National, 1937-1943.

Conde de Ficalho, *Garcia de Orta e o seu Tempo*, Lisboa, Imprensa National, 1886.

Congreso Provincial da India Portuguesa -subsidio para a sua Historia, ed. Antonio Maria da Cunha, 6 vols, Nova Goa, Casa Luso Francesa, 1924-1931.

Constituiçoes do Achebispado de Goa, ed. Dom Antonio Taveira de Neiva Brum, Lisboa, Imprensa Regia, 1910.

Correa Gaspar, *Lendas da India,* 4 vols, Lisboa, Typographia da Academia Real das Sciencias, 1858-1864.

Correia, A. C. Germano da Silva, *India Portuguesa— Prostituiçao e Profilaxia Anti-venerea —Historia Demografia Etnografia Hygiene e Profilaxia*, Bastora, Tipografia Rangel, 1938.

–, –, *Historia da Colonizaçao Portuguesa da India*, 6 vols.,Lisboa, 1943-58.

Costa A. Bruto da, *Goa sob a dominaçao Portuguesa*, Margao, Tipografia do Ultramar, 1897.

Cunha Gonsalves, L. da, "*Usos e Costumes dos Habitantes nao- Cristaos da India Portuguesa*, in *Estudos Coloniais I*, 1948-1949, pp. 49-67.

Dalgado, Sebastiao Rodolfo,*Florilegio de Porverbios Concanis*, Coimbra, Imprensa da Universidade, 1922.

Danvers, F. C., *The Portuguese in India*, 2 vols, London, 1894.

D'Costa, Anthony, *The Christianisation of the Goa Islands*, Bombay, Heras Institute, 1965.

D'Cunha Jean, "Prostitution in a Patriarchal Society: A critical review of the SIT act" *Economic Political Weekly*, XXII, n. 45, 7 Nov, 1987.

Della Valle, Pietro, *The Travels of Pietro della valle in India* ed. E. Grey, 2 vols, London, 1892.

Dellon, François, *Narraçao da Inquisiçao de Goa*, Tr. M.V. Abreu, Nova Goa, Imprensa National, 1866.

Direitos de Familia, Ediçoes Lex, Coimbra, Coimbra Editora, Ltd, 1955.

Disney, A. R., *Twilight of the Pepper Empire Portuguese Trade in South-west India in the Early Seventeenth Century*, London, Harvard University Press, 1978.

Documenta Indica ed., Josef Wicki, 18 vols. (1540-1597), Rome, Monumenta Historica Societatis Iesu, 1948-1988.

Documentaçao para Historia das Missoes do Padroado Portugues do Oriente: India, ed. A da Silva Rego, 12 vols, (1499-1582), Lisboa, Agencia Geral das Colonias, 1947-1958.

Documentaçao Ultramarina Portuguesa, ed., A. da Silva Rego, 5 vols., Lisboa, Centro de Estudos Historicos Ultramarinos, 1960-1970.

Documentos Remetidos da India ou Livros de Monçoes, vols. I-V, ed., Bulhao Pato,, Lisboa, *Academia real das Sciencias*, 1880-1935, vols. VI-X, ed. Antonio da Silva Rego, Lisboa, 1974-1982.

Early Travels in India of Ralph Fitch, ed. William Foster, London, Oxford University Press, 1921.

Early Travels in India, ed. J. Talboys Wheeler, Calcutta, 1956.

Ferreira Martins, J. F., *Historia da Misericordia de Goa*, 3 vols, Nova Goa, Imprensa Nacional, 1910-1914.

—*As Misericordias e as Orfas de El-Rei*, Lisboa, 1932.

Fonseca, J. N. da, *An Historical and Archaelogical Sketch of the City of Goa*, Bombay, Thacker and Co. Ltd, 1878, reprint New Delhi, Asian Educational Services, 1986.

Figueiredo, Propercia Correia Afonso de, *A Mulher na India Portuguesa*,

Nova Goa, Tip. Bragança, 1933.

Fryer, John, *A New Account of East India and Persia*, 3 vols, London, 1909-1915. Reprint. New Delhi, Asian Educational Services, 1992.

Felner, R. J. de Lima, *Subsidios para a Historia da India Portuguesa, Academia real das Sciencias*, 1868.

Goa Cultural Patterns, ed., Saryu Doshi, Bombay, Tata Press Limited, 1983.

Jung, Anees, *Unveiling India*, New Delhi, Penguin Books, 1992.

Goa Cultural Trends, ed. ,P.P. Shirodkar, Panjim-Goa, *Casa Packmaster*, 1988.

Goan Society Through the Ages, ed., B. S. Shastry, New Delhi, Asian Publication Services, 1987.

Gosh, Srabashi, "Birds in a cage" : Changes in Bengali Social Life as recorded in Autobiographies by Women", *EPW*, XXI, n. 43, 25 October, 1986.

History of Dharmasastra, ed. P.V. Kane, vols. I and II, Bhandarkar Oriental Research Institute, Poona, 1974.

Legislaçao do Estado da India, 1901-1961, Goa, Imprensa Nacional.

Livro do Pai dos Cristaos, ed. Josef Wicki, Lisboa, Centro de Estudos Historicos Ultramarinos, 1969.

O Oriente Portugues, 1906, Nova Goa, Imprensa Nacional, 1906.

Mandelbaum, David G., "Sex roles and Gender relations in North India", *EPW*, XXI, n. 46, 15 November,1986.

Manucci, Nicolou, *Storia do Mogor*, ed. W. Irwine, 4 vols, London, J. Murray, 1908, Reprint Calcutta, Editions Indian, 1965-1967.

Mazumdar, Vina, "Women's studies: Challenges to educational System", *EPW*, XVI, n. 20, 16 May, 1981.

Jahangir,B.K., "Women and Property in Rural Bangladesh", EPW, XXII, Sept 5-12, 1987.

Mendes, A. Lopes, *A India Portuguesa*, 2 vols, New Delhi, Asian Educational Services,1989 (Reprint).

Portugueses no Oriente ed., E. A. de Sa Nogueira Pinto Balsemao, 3 vols, Nova Goa, Imprensa Nacional, 1881-82.

Pearson, M.N., *Coastal Western India,Studies from the Portuguese records*,New Delhi, Concept Publishing Company, 1981.

–, –, *The New Cambridge History of India – The Portuguese in India*, Cambridge, Cambridge University, 1987.

Pereira, Antonio, *Konkani Oparinchem Bhanddar*, (The Treasure of Konkani Proverbs), Panjim, Gulab Publications,1985.

Pissurlenkar, Panduranga, *Goa Pre-Portugusa atraves dos escritores Lusitanos dos seculos XVI e XVII*, Lisboa, 1961.

Prasad, A.K., *Devadasi System in Ancient India — A study of temple Dancing girls of South India*, Delhi,H. K. Publishers and Distributors.

Rocha, Leopoldo, "What a chronicler missed about Santa Monica of Goa —Untold History of a Rebellion", Church Review, vol.xxvi, no.2, 1992.

Rao, Prakash and Nandini, *The Status of Women*, New Delhi, Heritage Publishers, 1985.

Roles and Rituals for Women, ed. Julia Leslie, New Delhi, Motilal Banarsidass Publishers Pvt. Ltd, 1992.

Sacred Books of the East — The laws of Manu ed., F. Max Muller, vol. XXV, New Delhi, Motilal Banarsidass, 1970.

Saldanha, M.J.G., *Historia de Goa*, 2 vols, Bastora(Goa), Tipografia Rangel, 1925-1926.

Recasting Women — Essays in Colonial History, ed., Kumkum Sangari and Sudesh Vaid, New Delhi, Crescent Printing Works Ltd, 1989.

Santa Maria, Agostinho de, *Historia da Fundaçao do Real Convento de Santa Monica da Cidade de Goa*, Lisboa, A. Pedro Galram, 1699.

Scamell, G.V., "The New World and Europe in the Sixteenth Century" *The Historical Journal*, XII, 3 (1989).

Schurhammer, G., *Francis Xavier:His Life, His Times*, II(India, 1541-45), Roma,1977

Silva Gracias, Fatima da, *Health and Hygiene in Colonial Goa, 1510-1961*, New Delhi, Concept Publishing Company, 1994

–, –, *Quality of Life in colonial Goa: Its Hygienic Expression (19th-20th centuries)* in *Essays in Goan History*, ed. Teotonio R. de Souza, New Delhi, Concept Publishing Company, 1989.

–, –, 'A Muther na Literateura Indo-Portuguesa – Diversas facetas de Sundorem A' in Mare Libercum no-9, Julho 1995, Lisboa.

Soares, J.P., *Bosquejo das Possessoes Portuguesas no Oriente*, Lisboa,1851.

Souza, Francisco de, *Oriente Conquistado a Jesu Christo pelos Padres da Compania de Jesus*, 2 vols,Bombay, Examiner Press, 1881-1886.

Souza, Caetano Francisco de, *Instituiçoes Portuguezas de Educaçao e Instruçao no Oriente*, vol I, Bombay, Job Printing Press, 1890.

Souza, Teotonio R. de, "The Afro-Asian Church in the Portuguese Estado da India" in Ogbu U. Kalu (ed.), *African Church Histography : An*

Ecumenical Perspective — Papers presented at a workshop on African Church History held at Nairobi, August 3-8, 1986, Berne, 1988.

–, –, "Norte -Sul no Estado da India", paper presented at Seventh International Seminar on Indo-Portuguese History, Goa 1994 .

Souza, Viterbo, *Portugueses e o gentio, Boletim do Instituto de Coimbra,* Coimbra, 1896.

Subrahmanyam, Sanjay, *The Portuguese Empire in Asia 1500-1700 – A Political and Economic History,* Longman group UK Limited, London,1993.

Subbamma, Malladi, *Women, Tradition and Culture,* New Delhi, Sterling Publishers Private Ltd, 1985.

Sumario Chronologico de Decretos diocesanos desde 1775-1899 — Decretos do arcebispo D. Francisco d'Assumpçao e Brito, ed., Manuel Joao d'Albuquerque, Bastora, Tipografia Rangel, 1900.

The Travels of the Abbe Carre in India and the Near East, 1672-1674, ed., Charles Fawcett, vol. I, New Delhi, Asian Educational Services, 1990.

The Voyage of John Huygen van Linschoten to the East Indies, ed. A.C. Burnell and P.A. Tiele, vol. 2, London, 1885. Reprint. New Delhi, Asian Educational Services, 1988.

Thevenot and Careri, *Indian Travels of Thevenot and Careri,* ed. Surendranath Sen, New Delhi, National Archives, 1949, (Reprint).

Viagem do Francisco Pyrard de Laval, ed., Magalhaes Basto, 2 vols, Porto, Tipografia Domingos de Oliveira, 1944.

Jean-Baptiste Tavernier's *Travels in India,* ed. Crooke William, 2 vols, reprint, Oriental Books Reprint Corporation, New Delhi, 1977.

Women in Indian Society — A Reader, ed. Rehana Ghadially, New Delhi, Sage Publications, 1988.

Women in India — Equality, social Justice and development, ed., Leelam Devasia and V.V. Devasia, New Delhi, Crescent Printing Works, New Delhi, 1990.

Whiteway, R.S., *The rise of Portuguese Power in India, 1497-1550,*New Delhi, Asian Educational Services 1989 (reprint).

Xavier, Filipe Nery, *Additamento do Codigo dos Usos e Costumes dos habitantes da Novas Conquistas,* Nova Goa, Imprensa National, 1861.

INDEX